The Book of Hindu Imagery

Ben Flynn

Other books by Binkey Kok Publications BV

Dirk Schellberg
Didgeridoo
Ritual Origins and Playing Techniques

Eva Rudy Jansen
The Book of Buddhas
Ritual Symbolism used
on Buddhist Statuary and Ritual Objects

Eva Rudy Jansen
Singing Bowls
A Practical Handbook of Instruction and Use

Ab Williams
The Complete Book of Chinese Health Balls
Background and Use of the Health Balls

George Hulskramer
The Life of Buddha
Prince Siddharta to Buddha

Töm Klöwer
The Joy of Drumming
Drums and Percussion Instruments from around the World

The Book of Hindu Imagery

The Gods and their Symbols

Compiled by: **Eva Rudy Jansen**

Binkey Kok Publications • Haarlem • The Netherlands

Tenth printing, 2008

Copyright © 1993 by Binkey Kok Publications, PO Box 317,
2000 AH Haarlem, The Netherlands
(e-mail: post@gottmer.nl)
Binkey Kok Publications is an imprint of Uitgeverij Altamira-Becht BV
and member of the Gottmer Publishing Group BV in Haarlem,
The Netherlands

Cover design: Jaap Koning
Cover photo: Harm Kuiper
Photo p. 110: Bert Wieringa
Photo p. 118: Barry Koperberg
Photo's p. 2, 56, 84, 90, 106, 128: Collection Royal Tropical Institute and
collection Meulenbeld, Amsterdam
Interior artwork and lay-out: Eva Rudy Jansen
Printing and binding: Bariet, Ruinen, The Netherlands

ISBN 978 90 74597 07 4

www.binkey-kok.com
www.altamira-becht.nl
www.diepmagazine.nl

Dedicated to

Shiva Nataraja
the god of the eternal cycle of creation

and his son

Ganesha
who removes all obstacles

Table of contents

Foreword

The valley of the Indus was inhabited as long ago as 2500 BC. Not much is known about the culture of the inhabitants, but it is clear that their religious feelings were directed towards the forces of nature, the sun, moon, earth, water, trees, mountains ...

This culture came to an abrupt end in about 1500 BC, when Indo-Aryan peoples moved to the area from the northwest. It was at this time that the religion now known as Hinduism first appeared.

In fact, Hinduism is more than a religion; it is at the same time a religion, a philosophy, and a way of life. In contrast with the other great world religions Hinduism as a religion is not based on a single holy book – there are many, all of equal importance – or on the words of one or more prophets. Hinduism is a culture in the widest sense of the word, and as a culture it grows in a way that could be described as organic, and is influenced by all the factors and circumstances which present themselves. It is like the river Ganges: a stream springs from a number of sources and is fed by other small streams as it flows along until it becomes a broad river which in turn divides into many small streams before flowing into the sea. In the same way, modern Hinduism is fed by countless sources, and branches out into a broad range of movements which are all important in their own way. Clearly it is not possible in such a small book as this to give a picture of such a complex subject as Hinduism which is in any way complete. In fact, this book does not aim to do so. Our aim was to provide a practical guide for the interested layman who encounters the magnificent classical artistic expressions of Hinduism (particularly in sculpture). In our opinion, the wealth and beauty of this art transcends even that of classical Greek art, which is justifiably highly valued in our culture.

In the West we have the opportunity to see increasing numbers of works of art and sculpture from classical Indian art and there is a growing interest in understanding what is seen. We have tried to meet this need for an understanding by providing a survey of the most important gods from the richly populated Hindu pantheon in the clearest possible way, and wherever we can we have included clearly illustrated points of identification for the countless manifestations of these gods. In this respect it is also impossible to be complete and we have not endeavoured to achieve this. Instead, we have tried to describe wherever possible something of the colourful background and the wealth of legend surrounding the different gods.

Publisher and compiler

Part 1

Introduction

Tempel in Khajuraho
Temple in Khajuraho

The Living Past

There probably is no other country in the world like India, where the history of the past three thousand years is revealed as clearly in the values and views of daily life. In this respect the sort of historical explanations used in the West are of minor importance. In fact, all the heroes and the heroic deeds from the (distant) past have been transformed into mythical figures and stories. Their significance lies not so much in the political influence they have had, as in the eternal principles of human frailty, strength, beauty and destiny, which they represent. For a Hindu, truth is unchanging, and it is of little importance how it is expressed and whether the specific form of expression came about a long time ago or whether it is created today.

On the basis of this principle, it is not only the history of mankind which has been transformed into a mythology which can still be used as a lesson and inspiration in daily life today; divine beings have also survived the centuries, constantly changing face and content. Every successive cultural development of human thought and feelings was incorporated in religious experience without rejecting the ancient principles and the deities linked with these. They changed appearance and sometimes became subordinate to their successors, but a Hindu today can still appeal to a god who was also revered by his ancestors three thousand years ago.

This organic growth, which is like a tree constantly producing more branches from the same roots, has turned Hinduism into a religion and a philosophy in which there is room, in principle, for everyone to have their own place.

The diversity of views and influences, and the absence of any obvious founder or an all-encompassing body of rules, have resulted in a view of human diversity which is characteristic of Hinduism as a whole. It is also the explanation for a number of phenomena which can all be traced back to the recognition of the large number of individual differences which exist between people.

For example, in religious practice there are a number of different paths which are equally valued and which can be followed to reach the divine goal of salvation from the cycle of rebirth. Each person has his own character and talents. For a person with a philosophical bent the path of knowledge (*jnana*), is the correct path, while for a person with a practical bent it is the path of deeds (*karma*), for a disciplined person, the path of spiritual self-control (*yoga*) and for a devout person, it is the path of worship (*bhakti*).

Every life is divided into four stages which a person could ideally follow in order to fulfil his religious obligations satisfactorily. These stages of life (*ashramas*) are: *brahmacarya*, the stage of discipline and education, the youthful years; *garhasthya*, the stage of parenthood and active work in which worldly ties are loosened; the young adult; *vanaprasthya*, the stage of retreat in which worldly ties are loosened; middle age; and *sannyasa*, the life of a hermit, old age. From the social point of view a recognition of human diversity is one of the basic concepts which still supports the historically developed caste system. The religious and philosophical idea behind this system is that every person has an individual place and task to fulfil in society, which are the result of his past lives and a way into the next, possibly better life. The historical background can be traced back to the time when the Aryans moved into the valley of the Indus. Already, India was populated by different races, such as the dark Dravidians in the South, and the inhabitants of the Indus valley with their highly developed culture in the North; these were now joined by the warlike Aryans. This diversity of cultures, philosophies and ideas undoubtedly encouraged the distinction between the classes which finally resulted in the rigid caste system. There were the castes of the brahmins (priests), kshatriyas (warriors), vaishyas (merchants) and shudras (labourers) and below these the pariahs or untouchables.

What applied to men also applied to the gods. There are many, each with their own place and significance. But this place in the pantheon and the significance of any particular god are constantly changing. When a particular god is the focus of devotion and worship, he or she is always the greatest and the most important, Mahadeva, the father, mother or lord of all other gods. At that moment all the others are subordinate to him or her. At first, this may seem confusing and give rise to the question who is actually the Only True One, the Great God. However, this question is irrelevant. There are many magnificent tales about the battles for supremacy between the gods, but these are merely expressions of human rivalry. In divine reality every god and every manifestation of that god is an aspect of the great indivisible whole. Though Hinduism may appear to be pantheistic, ultimately everything centres around the One Divine Truth, the fundamental principle of creation, which, like creation itself, has so many aspects that every facet of that creation, every person and every human principle is reflected in it.

The god who is the object of devotion at any particular time is therefore just one of the many different faces which are turned to us and address us. Therefore, it is only the most important for that particular moment.

The Holy Books

There are a variety of methods for classifying gods in a survey of the most important gods and a number of their manifestations.

One way is to start with the gods which are most important now, or the most well known, and then to show which gods are associated with them and which preceded them.

In this book we have used another method, viz., a chronological classification based on the historical periods of development.

Though the principles of Hinduism may be timeless, there has nevertheless been a development in time which has resulted not only in the present religious pluriformity, but which is also reflected in the artistic treasures which have survived centuries of war, pillage, natural disasters and other wear and tear.

Several main periods can be distinguished in this historical development of Hinduism.

First of all, there was the period of the civilization in the valley of the Indus. It is known that this already existed in about 2500 BC. There are both art treasures and written works extant from this highly developed civilization, though the latter have not yet been (completely) deciphered. It is assumed that during this period natural phenomena were experienced as divine forces, though no human form was ascribed to them. Traces of animal and snake worship have been discovered, as well as of the worship of a Mother Goddess.

With the invasion of the Indo-Aryans in about 2000 BC, this civilization came to an abrupt end. In religious life, natural forces gradually assumed a human form. The world was populated by natural spirits, and anthropomorphic gods made an appearance.

In this period lays the origination of the Vedas, a number of holy texts with different contents and of a different nature which are written down between approximately 1200 BC (the Rig-Vedas) and 400 BC (the later Upanishads). The oral tradition goes back to 2000 BC and before. In broad terms, the Vedas are subdivided into three parts: the *Samhitas*, songs of praise exalting the gods (Rig-Veda), and the accompanying melodies (Sama-Veda) and sacrificial formulae (Yayur-Veda); the *Brahmanas*, texts dealing with sacrifices and rituals as they should be carried out by priests, and their meaning; and the *Aranyakas* and the *Upanishads*, philosophical and mystical treatises on the nature of the Highest Reality.

The gods, products of the humanization of natural forces are the most important subject of the Vedas and the focus of acts of atonement and penance. The destiny of man is in the hands of the gods, everything must be done to appease them, and only priests (brahmins) can serve as intermediaries.

Gradually this sacrificial culture was replaced by a new view – the idea of the Brahman, the Supreme, all-permeating Divine Principle, and of the Atman, the manifestation of this principle in the human soul, the Self. Man acquired a more central position and the practice of sacrifice was gradually supplemented or replaced by the practice of devotion (bhakti).

This was the time of the great epic books (from approx. 400 BC to approx. 600 AD): the *Ramayana*, the *Mahabharata* and the most famous part of this, the *Bhagavad Gita*. These stories, which are all based on the mythical inner battle which man(kind) is constantly waging in choosing between good and evil, the gods assume extremely human forms and man has the opportunity of touching the divine aspect of himself.

600 BC was the beginning of the period when great temples were built, and a time of development of various movements in the practice of divine worship. There was also a new series of religious books, the *Puranas*, the "ancient stories". These give a summary of all the familiar gods with their descendants, and provide religious instructions regarding the ways in which the gods can be served and worshipped. Three movements are indicated with their main gods, together forming the "three in one" (Trimurti): Brahma, Vishnu and Shiva. In addition, there was the Shakta movement which was focussed on the mother goddess. This was the time of the creation of the works of art which are still so impressive today. Large temple complexes were

built, filled inside and out with magnificent sculptures.

A careful observation of nature and natural phenomena had soon led to the important conclusion that no material phenomenon remains unchanged for all eternity. Everything in the universe is subject to constant change and therefore any individual movement is imperfect. In order to express a perfect version of a divine principle one should therefore not attempt to copy nature. That is why a representation of a deity consists of a summary of principles and characteristics represented in accordance with strict rules. The pose, clothes, hairstyle, attributes and symbols surrounding the god all relate a message which can be translated by devout believers into the divine principle which is represented by this pictorial summary.

In this extremely materialistic representation of a divine principle one can recognize and worship the immaterial god. In this way, images of gods are worshipped and cared for as though they were alive.

It is not only sculptures made by human hands that reflect the divine principle. Phenomena and forms which occur spontaneously in nature can also reflect the gods in this way. Thus a mountain peak represents the male sexual organ, the lingam; while a chasm between the rocks represents the female sexual organ, the yoni. The act of copulation, in which these two elements become one, represents the removal of all contrasts, such as birth and death, man and woman, good and evil, the beginning and the end, god and demon. This fusion, which can be experienced by anyone in the sexual act between a man and a woman, leads to the liberation of consciousness from the illusion of duality. It integrates the body and the mind, or in other words, reunites the cosmic will with the material forms in which this expresses itself. The practice of ritual eroticism and the erotic representations in the temples merely serve to achieve and express this Unio Mystica, this mystical Unification of Opposites.

In addition to the visual images created by man and nature as a pictogram of a divine principle, Hindu iconography also has a series of geometric symbols and diagrams which express or accommodate a divine principle. The principle of male and female energy and their unification is often expressed in the geometric patterns illustrated here. The two upper figures represent the female principle (double yoni) and the three following symbols represent the male prin (lingam, spearhead and flame). The last three diagrams are all bols of the principle of creation, of the unification of the two f

Just as a god can manifest himself in countless forms, a god can also appear in any place which pleases him/her, and in this way turn this place into a site for ritual acts. A god can be invited to descend to a particular place by means of special diagrams, so that he can be worshipped there. Drawing such a **yantra** is in itself a holy act. The divine principle is contained in the yantra, which is represented on a two-dimensional plane, though it is three-dimensional in reality. The yantra illustrated here is the **shrichakra** or **shriyantra**. An equilateral triangle serves as the symbol for the unattainable, the divine. The overlapping triangles represent the male and female principles. The point in the middle represents eternity. The square is the symbol of the earth; two squares, one within the other, symbolize heaven and earth together.

Holy formulae or *mantras* are chanted when the yantra is drawn and the god is summoned. These consist of ordinary words, syllables and sounds which must be uttered in a special order, at a special pitch and in a special rhythm. The Vedic syllable, OM, is considered the holiest mantra of all.

Part 2

The Language of the Gods

The Images Speak

In Hinduism, an image of a god is a direct symbol of the god himself. Perhaps it would be more accurate to say that in the image of the god we can see the spirit of the god. Thus, when the image is prayed to, worshipped and cared for with ritual acts such as bathing, feeding and clothing, it is in fact the god himself who is served in this way.

In the same way that we can approach the gods through their images, the gods can speak to us through the same channel.

All the parts and characteristics of a particular image have a special meaning. By means of a pose, gesture, clothing and attributes, the image reveals which aspect the god is showing us and from which identity he/she is approaching, which story from the rich mythological history is being brought to our attention.

This narrative style using poses and gestures can also be seen in the elaborate Indian art of dancing; not only the movements of the body, arms and legs, but also subtle changes in the angle of an eyebrow or the movement of a finger, help to express a mood, an aspect or a particular act. Anyone who learns this language can not only identify a particular god by his characteristic pose and external identifying marks, but can also tell in which of his – in some cases – many manifestations the god is appearing. This chapter and the next contain a brief description of this "language of the gods".

Positions of the body

The pose which a god assumes (**asana**) shows at a glance whether this god is in a relaxed mood, or in an aggressive or contemplative mood. His or her position can also indicate a particular act or be a reference to a feat of arms.

Samabhanga

Literally: without bending. The normal starting position for standing representations. The god stands with his weight spread equally over his two feet, his body erect in tranquil equilibrium.

A variation of this asana is **sthanu**, the "pillar position", (see illustration). This is the petrified position, e.g., of Shiva as an ascetic, when he stands deep in meditation for such a long time that one universe ends and another is created. Thus, another name for this aspect of Shiva is, Sthanu, "he who stands like a pillar."

Abhanga

This standing position in which the body weight is supported by one leg, both feet standing on the ground, with knees stretched and the hip pushed out on the side which is not supporting the weight, represents the fact that the god is deep in thought. The word "abhanga" means: with one curve. There are also the "dvibhanga" and the "tribhanga", respectively positions with two and three curves (hips, shoulders and neck), which indicate a beneficent mood, and the "atibhanga", the tribhanga with sharp curves in the hips and shoulders, which indicates violent movement or sometimes even violence. This is Shiva's position in some of his destructive aspects.

Padasvastika

The weight is supported on one leg, while the other leg is crossed in front of it, lightly supported by the toes. It is a position which represents benevolent tranquillity and relaxation and which is particularly common for Krishna when he is playing the flute.

Alidhapada

The two feet stand firmly on the ground. The left leg is slightly stretched back, while the right leg is placed in front with bent knee. This is the position of an archer, characteristic of Shiva and others in their role of destroyer of the three cities. Another name is "alidham". When the left leg is bent forwards, the position is known as "pratyalidham" and expresses rage and pugnacity.

Padmasana

The lotus position. The feet are crossed, the toes are placed in the groin. This is the position of deep meditation.

Yogasana

The yogi position. The legs are crossed with the feet touching the ground. The knees are slightly drawn up and supported by a special tape (yogapatta). This position shows a god as an ascetic. In a variation of this position, only the right leg is drawn up and supported by the yogapatta while the left leg hangs down.

Virasana

This "heroic position" is found in several different forms. One of these is hardly any different from the padmasana. The legs are placed on top of each other instead of being intertwined. In many cases just one leg lies curved on the pedestal, while the other hangs down to the ground. This position represents a god who has revealed himself to be a hero in the battle against the demons.

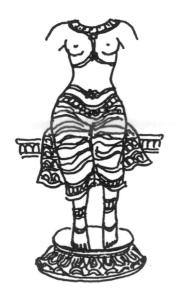

Pralambapadasana

The "European" position. It looks as though the god is seated on a chair, both legs hang down and the feet are resting on the ground. This position indicates that the god is deep in contemplation.

Rajalilasana

The "royal", playful position. This is a relaxed position which is often seen in gods who are represented seated next to their wife. One leg is drawn up, the other hangs down quite relaxed and the weight of the body is often supported by the arm (slightly stretched back). If both legs are drawn up, this is no longer a "royal" position but is known as "lilasana".

Nrityamurti

This is the position of a god engaged in a dance. The dancer stands on one leg, with a slightly bent knee, while the other leg is supported with the foot against the inside of the thigh of the standing leg.

Dance is seen as the ultimate universal act of creation when a god is dancing, and as a form of magic when a person dances. In this case the dancer assumes the personality of the god who is depicted as he is dancing.

Examples of dancing gods include: Shiva-Nataraja, Krishna on the snake, Kaliya, and Ganesha as Nritya-Ganapati.

Surrounding elements

Divine feet never touch the ground on earth; gods are not subject to worldly laws, but only to the cosmic cycle. Non-divine beings, such as demons and spirits, do not have any special place for sitting and standing; a god has a seat or a pedestal which can even be seen as the dwelling place of that god, and thus in itself as a sacred object.

The geometric shape of a divine seat has a different meaning depending on the symbolism of the shape and numbers.

Sometimes the shape is even composed of a number of different shapes stacked one above the other, such as the **bhadrapitha**, a square with a circle above it. If a pedestal has a single, clearly identifiable shape, this also indicated one specific aspect of the god; if several forms are used together in one pedestal, this is for a more unusual representation of the god.

Gods are often depicted in a nimbus which surrounds the whole figure. This halo, or **prabhamandala**, is often decorated with a pattern of leaves originating from the sacred tree, the symbol of cosmic power. Sometimes there is a clearly identifiable circle of flames, as in the dancing god Shiva Nataraja.

An arch supported by two pillars often serves as a connecting element for one image or group of images. It symbolizes the gate from the earthly to the heavenly regions. The arches are always lavishly decorated, with patterns of plants, symbols, creatures, and often with the ultimate crown of a mask, or **kirtimukha**, which provides divine protection.

Padmapitha

Lotus pedestal; also known as **padmasana** and identified by the lotus leaves around the feet. The lotus is the symbol of a mother's lap, amongst other things. All of life originates from this, including the life of the gods. That is why padmapitha is one of the most highly valued pedestals.

Temple imagery can be divided into five groups. The geometric pattern of a particular pedestal shows what a god is doing at a particular time. For example there is:

Arcabera – images intended for worship by devout believers; they have a hexagonal pedestal or seat.

Autsavabera – images which accompany a particular festival.

Balibera – images which accept sacrifices; hexagonal pedestal or seat.

Dhruvabera – images which are permanently placed in the temple.

Snapanabera – images which are intended for bathing, square pedestal or seat.

In addition, a hexagonal seat indicates that a god is relaxed and observing some form of entertainment; the octagonal seat is for images which accompany an initiation ritual, and the round or oval seat is the specific meditation throne.

Hand positions

In all the visual arts, from painting to dance, gestures (**mudra**) play an important role. It is literally the "language of gestures of the gods" with which they clearly express their intentions, emotions and qualities in a very sophisticated way.

Abhaya
The right hand raised with the palm of the hand facing forwards. This indicates blessing, protection and reassurance.

Jnana
The hand is placed level with the heart with the palm facing upwards. The thumb forms a ring, usually with the ring finger. This is the gesture of wisdom, as a quality of the god concerned.

Tarjani
The raised index finger expresses a threat or warning.

Varada
The left hand, with the fingers pointing downwards, points toward the believer with an open palm, indicating that the god is prepared to grant a wish or bestow a blessing.

Vismaya
This is the gesture of surprise or wonder which a god makes only when he recognizes the superiority of another god who is present.

Vitarka

With this gesture, in which the thumb and index finger form a ring, the god proves his pure judgement and intellectual wisdom.

If he stretches out his hand to the observer, this means he wishes to give instruction.

Anjali

The hands are loosely held together with the palms together and the fingers stretched up.

If they are held in this position in front of the chest, this denotes worship. If they are held in front of the forehead, the gesture can also be a greeting (**Namaskara**).

Dhyana

The god sits in a position of meditation and places the right hand inside the left hand in the lap with the palms turned up. This position, also known as **yogamudra**, indicates a condition of deep meditation.

Gestures of hand and arm
(Hastas)

Gaja

The arm is stretched diagonally across the chest with the fingers pointing down. This gesture symbolizes an elephant's trunk: it is a sign of the greatest strength and power. It is seen above all in Shiva-Nataraja.

Hastasvastika

The arms crossed in front of the chest indicate total surrender to a god with a superior position.

Pataka

The arm is stretched like the wing of a bird, symbolizing strength. Sometimes this gesture also refers to the power of flames in a fire.

Damaru

This gesture and the following three do not have any symbolic significance of their own. These gestures are so closely related to the symbolic objects they are holding that they are often illustrated without those objects, assuming the symbolism of the object.

Damaru-hasta is the gesture with which the drum, damaru, is held.

Kataka

Holding a lotus flower; this position of the hand invites the believer to make the gift of a flower.

Ardhacandra

This is the gesture with which the god carries fire either with or without a fire dish.

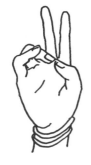

Kartari

Attributes are often held with this gesture.

If the gesture is made without an attribute between the outstretched index and middle finger, it symbolizes the antlers of a deer, representing the contradictions inherent in all things.

Headdresses and hairstyles

One of the striking aspects of the illustrations of Hindu gods, particularly in Indian art, is the wealth of decoration of the headdress or crown. Sometimes it is difficult to distinguish the crown from the tall entwined tresses of hair, often more difficult than the difference between one headdress (crown) and another (turban).

Nevertheless, it is precisely these external characteristics such as headdresses and hairstyles, as well as ornaments and garments, which provide a great deal of information about the god wearing them. In illustrations the subtle differences are sometimes difficult to distinguish, and therefore we will not examine them in great detail here. However, it would be useful to mention some of the most common crowns and hairstyles. Some information about these matters can be very useful for recognizing the main gods.

Headdresses

Shirastraka
Turban of cloth or braided tresses of hair tied in a knot at the front. This is worn by subsidiary figures in the company of the gods, by demons and celestial creatures.

Kiritamukuta

Literally and metaphorically, the highest of all crowns. The shape is that of a rather conical cylinder, similar to a mitre, ending in a knot or point. This is the crown worn by Vishnu and all the gods which can be related to him.

When it is worn by a goddess, this is the sign that the goddess has the same rank as the highest gods at that moment.

Jatamukuta

A crown of artfully plaited braids, which is reminiscent of the shape of the kiritamukuta, and is often just as lavishly decorated. Jatamukuta is the crown of an ascetic. It is worn particularly by Shiva (though in fact not when he is depicted as an ascetic), with a sickle or skull as the characteristic ornament, and by Brahma, decorated with jewels.

Karandamukuta

This crown is smaller than the kiritamukuta and tapers to a point like a pile of plates in narrower and narrower layers.

A god or goddess who is wearing this crown, in this way shows his subordinate position in the pantheon.

Hairstyles

The way in which the hair is worn without a crown also reveals a great deal about the qualities of the figure which is depicted.

The names distinguish between smooth long hair (**kesha**) and plaited hair (**jata**).

The hairstyle of goddesses is always an indication of their place in the hierarchy at that moment. They often wear their hair tied up in a high topknot, with either straight or plaited hair (**keshabandha** or **jata-bandha**) and decorated with jewels. If the topknot is smoother or lower, or tied together at the side (**dhammilla**), this means that the figure is a goddess or a member of her retinue who has a subordinate position at that time.

Demons are sometimes depicted with a hairstyle which is almost identical in shape to a turban (**shirastraka**).

The god Shiva, who has more manifestations than any other Hindu god, is depicted in his various aspects with a great variety of different crowns and hairstyles. Thus his headdress is often an excellent means of identifying the particular manifestation.

For example, he appears with the name **Kaparda**, a reference to the shape of the hairstyle which he has in this manifestation; with penitential braids wound round his head in a spiral like a snail's shell. Another of his characteristic hairstyles is that of the fan of penitential braids of Shiva the dancer, Shiva-Nataraja (see illustration). In many cases they are decorated with snakes.

Jatabhara

Shiva's hairstyle illustrated on the previous page is a special form of the jatabhara hairstyle. The word means "burden of braids" and the hairstyle is usually characterized by a large number of penitential plaits worn in a bunch on the side, as in Shiva-Daksina-Murti.

Jatamandala

When a god appears in one of his/her terrifying manifestations, this can sometimes be identified by the hairstyle away from the head with a circle of smooth hair (keshamandala) or penitential braids (jatamandala) around the head.

Jvalakesha

The word means "flaming hair", and the hairstyle consists of hair which is worn straight up or all round the head, curling like flames. This hairstyle is characteristic of the fire god, Agni, and is also worn by the goddess Kali.

Garments

The way in which the gods' garments are represented is influenced to some extent by different eras and artists' individual ideas. There are also slight differences between garments depicted in the south and the north of India. Nevertheless, there are qualities which can usually be identified, like those parts of the clothing which have a symbolic significance and these are therefore always illustrated.

In most classical works of art there is very little clothing, though the few garments are richly decorated with ornaments etc. The garments worn on the lower part of the body are generally generously pleated, but nevertheless close around the legs, with some differences between the male (**kaccha**) and female (**dukula**) garments. In some cases this garment, which reaches just above the ankles, is replaced by a short, but equally richly decorated loincloth (**kaupina**). This garment is tied with a striking belt by both men and women.

Apart from their ornaments, male gods have a bare torso, while goddesses usually wear a cloth around the breasts.

Vishnu wears a special garment (**pitambara**). This is made of gold and symbolizes the Vedas: the light of truth radiates through the holy words, just as the divine light of Vishnu shines through his garment. When a god is illustrated unclothed, this means he is appearing in the manifestation of an ascetic, e.g., Shiva, who sometimes wanders around dressed as a beggar, covered in white ashes and wearing only sandals.

Belts

A belt worn by a goddess, is usually called **katisutra**. When it consists of eight separate bands it is called **mekhala**. This mekhala provides protection as well as fertility, and was therefore used in the past in special rituals to beg the gods for rain, or conversely, for protection against flooding.

The belts of male gods are usually called **katibandha**. This looks more like a hipband than a belt around the waist. Often it is completely decorated with lions' heads and snake designs.

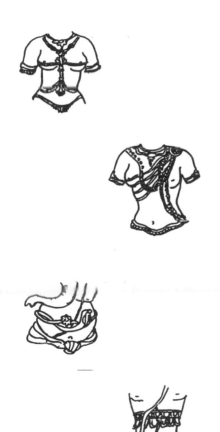

Breast bands

In illustrations from the south of India goddesses often wear a supporting cloth around the breasts, attached to the decorative ornament around the neck (**kucabandha**) with one or more vertical straps. In northern India several cloths are worn around the breasts, or one cloth is worn diagonally (**stanottariya**).

Terrifying goddesses and demons wear a snake as a breast cloth, which raises its head from between her breasts and peers threateningly at the observer. Male gods, specially Krishna and Ganesha, often wear a broad belt, **udarabandha**, below the ribs. In Ganesha this also sometimes takes the form of a snake. The cloth which Shiva-Nataraja wears around the chest is called **urassutra**.

The sacrificial cord

Every boy in the three highest castes undergoes an initiation ritual at the beginning of puberty (Upanayana or Janeu). This is comparable in importance to baptism in Christianity. The name Janeu refers to part of the ceremony: the boy receives a sacrificial cord consisting of three intertwined strands as long as an adult man. The three strands represent the three Gunas (fundamental qualities of matter): sattva (reality), rajas (passion) and tamas (inertia). The solemn ceremony heralds the start of a new stage of life: the boy is reborn and is now a man.

This cord, which is worn in a loop around the left shoulder and right hip, is always part of the clothing of the gods, both male and female. The usual name for the cord is **yajnopavita**.

The material and style of the sacrificial cord always correspond to the other garments of the god concerned and the aspect in which he/she is appearing. Materials which are commonly used include fabric (**vastrayanopavita**) and antelope hide (**ajinayaianopavita**). The cord may be lavishly decorated, often with jewels, particularly when the god is illustrated in a festive aspect. Goddesses often wear garlands of flowers as a sacrificial cord.

When they appear in a terrifying aspect, the gods have human skulls hanging from their cord.

Some of the gods who wear their own characteristic cord include ̅ha, with a cord of snakes (**valayajnopavita**) and Shiva, who ̅cobra as a sacrificial cord (**sarpayajnopavita**) when he ap-̅as a naked yogi.

Ornaments

Originally people wore amulets which were meant to protect the part of the body on which they were worn against disease and other afflictions, or were otherwise worn to give it a special power. As these amulets were more and more richly decorated, they became ornaments. The ornaments worn by the Hindu gods directly reflect a deeper significance in their form, again of course also reflecting the particular aspect of the god – whether this is benevolent or terrifying. When the gods wear ornaments where they are also worn by man, there is often a remarkable difference in the materials used compared with "human" ornaments. For depending on the particular aspect of the god which is illustrated, the ornaments can consist of flowers, berries, wood, silver, gold, precious stones, pearls and snakes, but also of scorpions, teeth, bones and skulls.

Sometimes there are special symbols or emblems which still directly reveal the principle of a talisman or amulet. Ornaments can be divided into diadems, necklaces and garlands (**mala**), earrings (**kundala**), other ornaments for the ears (**avatansa**), rings for the fingers, bracelets (**valaya**) and anklets (**padasara**). All these ornaments can be worn by both male and female gods. In many cases there is little difference between the ornaments worn by men and women. However, there are certain sorts which are considered specifically male or female. This applies particularly to earrings (see below).

Mala

In the West this term has become familiar in connection with the prayer beads, usually made of wood, which are used by the followers of Indian gurus (Osho, Maharishi Mahesh Yogi).

The general meaning of the word is "chain" of any sort.

As the prayer beads (**akshamala**) are usually used as an attribute, they are described in that chapter. In this chapter we will mention some of the ornaments worn around the neck which are related to a special aspect of the god. There is a particularly large variety of these worn by female gods, such as precious stones which have been strung together (**ratnamala**), flowers (**vanamala**) or beads, simply known as **mala**.

Special ornaments worn around the neck with large gems set in gold, indicate a benevolent aspect of the goddess. In the course of time this chain (**phalakahara**) has become longer and longer, until it hangs down to the belly with a heavy pendant (**lambaka**).

Supporters of different Hindu sects believe that the strength of the gods resides in the chain which belongs to them. For example, the chain of the god Indra protects him and grants victory in battle.

The chains offered to a god or worn by believers themselves reveal the sect to which the believer belongs. For example, followers of Vishnu can be identified by garlands of flowers. Chains made of a special sort of seed (**raksha**, also known as **rudraksha**) are also popular. The number of ribs on the seed indicates to which god or which principle the chain is dedicated (in most cases, this is Shiva).

Ornaments for the ears

Just as every Hindu boy receives a sacrificial cord when he is initiated into adulthood, a girl has her ears pierced for this occasion, so that she can wear earrings.

Wearing ornaments in the ears, especially earrings, is therefore the privilege and sign of someone "who has been born for the second time." The more ornate, i.e., the heavier the ornament in the ears, the more it will stretch the earlobes. Thus elongated earlobes have become a sign of power, nobility and wealth.

It is not surprising that gods have richly decorated ears and long earlobes.

There is a distinction between ornaments of different materials, such as flowers, and chains which are worn around the ears (**avatansa**), and earrings which are worn in the pierced earlobe (**kundala**). Again male and female gods both wear the various different sorts, though there are some which are considered specifically male or female.

A specifically male ornament is the snake earring (**sarpakundala**). This is worn particularly by Shiva (in his right ear) and Ganesha. Goddesses wear this ring as a sign of their power when they are depicted independently, and not in their subordinate role as a subsidiary figure with a male god.

Some truly female ornaments include the broad, smooth ring made of gold leaf (**pattrakundala**), the shell ring (**sankhapattrakundala**) and the ring with the shape of a long, golden leaf (**lampapattra**). These earrings are worn by goddesses and also by Shiva in his left ear when he wishes to emphasize his androgynous nature.

Ganesha, an example of rich ornamentation

Part 3

Symbols and Attributes

Symbol, Emblem, Attribute

Long before natural phenomena and divine power were depicted in human form as gods, these principles had already been illustrated, usually in geometric patterns. There is often a striking resemblance between these **symbols** as they are used all over the world. The wheel of the sun is a good example of this.

A similar human tendency is to represent an idea, property or quality in the form of an object, plant, animal or something else which is considered to possess the particular quality or property concerned. With regard to these **emblems** there are obviously greater differences between various cultures than there are between the symbols in their purest form. (Examples: the Christian olive branch, the Hindu/Buddhist lotus flower).

Regardless of the way in which they are depicted, Hindu gods are always surrounded by symbols and emblems. In addition, they often hold in their hands a variety of attributes which each individually represents a particular divine power or quality. A god who wishes to reveal a great number of qualities and powers at the same time therefore has a greater number of hands. In this way we can tell, even more clearly than from the clothes and ornaments, in which form and with which specific power(s) and strength(s) the god is appearing at that moment.

The following pages give a survey of common symbols, emblems and attributes, wherever possible accompanied by their English name to identify them and to facilitate classification.

Antelope
(Mriga) In Vedic times antelope skin was an important part of every religious ritual. The antelope was considered the most powerful animal. In South Indian art, Shiva is depicted with an antelope on his left hand, as a sign that he is the lord of nature (natural forces).

Axe
(Parashu) The weapon that conquers the dark and ignorance and in this way liberates man from the ties of all worldly matters. It is a characteristic attribute of Shiva, Ganesha and, as a battle axe, of the war god, Skanda.

Banner
(Dhvaja) In the hands of a god, a banner is a weapon. In a temple to Shiva, the banner, pillar and flag pole have the same symbolic significance: the flaming lingam of the god himself. Worshipping the banner brings good luck.

Begging bowl

(Bhikshapatra) Gods in the manifestation of a wandering ascetic carry this bowl with them. (Brahma, Shiva, Ganesha). The bowl is sometimes difficult to distinguish from the *skull bowl* and the sacrificial bowl (patra).

Bell

(Ghanta) Symbol of the mystical primal sound which is the origin of creation. All musical instruments are united in the sound of the bell. The bell is a characteristic attribute of Shiva and his wife, Kali. In the hand of Durga the bell is a weapon, and the sound inspires fear in all his enemies.

Bolt of Lightning

(Vajra) The symbol of invulnerability and invincibility. As a weapon it drives ⟨
Originally it was th
Indra, and was usu
as a sort of double-
In later times it b
"diamond sceptre'

Book
(Pustaka) This sign of wisdom refers to the Vedic writings. The spoken and written word is seen as the origin of all of existence, and therefore the book often lies in the symbol of the mother's lap, the lotus. It is a special attribute of Brahma, his wife Sarasvati, and Vishnu.

Bow and arrow
(Bana-Dhanus) The arrow represents the male and the bow represents female energy. In addition, the arrow symbolizes the power of love, while the bow represents the death wish. The five arrows of the god of love, Kama, represent the five senses. The bow of a specific god often has its own name.

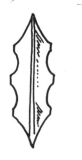

Chisel
(Tarika) Sometimes comparable to the axe (e.g., with Shiva and Durga); sometimes it also has the same symbolic significance as the spear. It is a special attribute of Subrahmanya, or a manifestation of the war god, Skanda.

Club
(Gada) One of the oldest weapons. This provides protection for the wearer and is at the same time a symbol of the power of natural laws and time, which destroys everything in its way. It is often depicted as a pestle. This is an attribute of Kali, Shiva, Ganesha and Skanda.

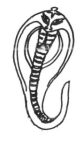

Cobra
(Naga) In Northern India, Shiva is always depicted with a trident and cobra (also see under *Snake*).

Conch shell
(Sankha) This is used as a musical instrument; the sound is a weapon to ward off demons. The conch shell is one of the main attributes of Vishnu. The spiralling in the conch is symbolic of infinite space, which constantly expands in a clockwise direction. If the conch spirals in an anti clockwise direction, the law nature have been reverse the shell belongs to Shiva

Dagger
(Churi) The dagger is always illustrated symbolizing a sacrificial knife. It is depicted particularly with goddesses in their terrifying manifestations, such as Durga and Kali.

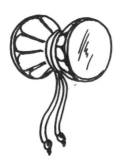

Drum
(Damaru) This is a typical attribute of Shiva as a dancer. The sound of the drum symbolizes the original sound which is the beginning of all things, the rhythm and vibrating strength of creation.

Feather
(Mayurapattra) Like the bird itself, peacock feathers are a symbol of immortality. They are more often depicted as an emblem than as an attribute, particularly with Shiva in some of his aspects as a dancer, and with gods who belong with him, such as Skanda.

Fire
(Agni) Fire is one of the oldest divine forces. In Vedic times, sacrifices were made to fire as to a god. As an attribute, it is a symbol of destruction, a condition of the creation of new life. It is seen particularly with Shiva, Durga, Kali and Agni.

Fly whisk
(Chamara) The brush of yak hair is a weapon which repels undesirable vermin, particularly for the goddess Ganga. For another goddess it can be a sign of her subordinate position. However, as an attribute of Vishnu, it is a sign of royalty and the attribute becomes a lucky talisman.

Food
(Modaka) Ganesha often has some form of food with him: biscuits, a sweet spicy flour-ball, or fruit (phala). Fruit in some form is always an attribute of Bala-Ganapati, Ganesha as a child.
The conical fruit of the Bilva tree symbolizes Shiva's lingam.

Hook
(Ankusha) In India this hook is used to give commands to elephants. In the hands of a god it is a sign of action and the ability to distinguish spiritual motives and steer them. It is a characteristic attribute of Ganesha and Skanda.

Lasso
(Pasha) The lasso is a symbol of an attachment to worldly matters, as well as the capacity of the god concerned to capture evil and (blind) ignorance. It is one of the most common attributes of Ganesha.

Lingam
(also: linga) The male sexual organ, symbol of the god Shiva and his omnipotence. The cylindrical shape was originally the symbol of the formlessness of nature. As a representation of clear consciousness, it is often depicted in many different ways together with the *yoni* (the female sexual organ and symbol of the origin of creation).

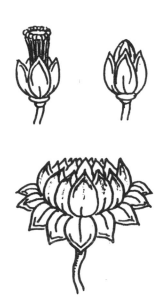

Lotus

(Padma) Every part and stage of this water plant has its own significance.

Stem: all of life comes from water. Leaf: the fertile earth. Flower: the mother's lap. Bud: virginity. Open flowers: the sun. The whole flower: symbol of beauty, happiness and eternal renewal. The throne of the gods is a lotus flower. As an attribute the lotus is depicted mainly with Surya, Vishnu and Lakshmi. In Northern India, it is usually depicted as an open flower, in southern India, it is shut.

Mirror

(Darpana) The mirror represents the aspect of Shiva that is not manifest. In his androgynous aspect he carries a mirror in one of his left hands (the female side). The mirror, as a symbol of wisdom, and at the same time of the emptiness of all worldly matters, is one of the specific attributes of female gods, such as Durga, particularly in their terrifying manifestations.

Mongoose
(Nakula) Symbol of wealth and abundance, it spews out jewels in the hands of the god of wealth, Kubera. The mongoose is the guardian of the snakes who in their turn guard all the riches of the earth.

Parasol
(Chattra) Ancient sign of royal power; in this function it is used particularly by the Vedic gods, Varuna and Surya. It gives protection, joy and luck, and is therefore the symbol of Vaikuntha, the paradise of Vishnu. It is also an attribute of Ganesha and Vamana.

Prayer beads
(Akshamala) The symbol of the eternal cycle of time. The material of which the beads are made depends on the aspect, in which the god who has the prayer beads is appearing. Often they are made of seeds (rudraksha); but they can also be made of pearls, skulls and discs of bone.
This is a special attribute of Brahma and Sarasvati.

Shield

(Khetaka) This gives protection against enemy attacks when it is in the hands of gods fighting against opponents of their own calibre. A god who has an invincible weapon never carries a shield - he/she does not need one.

Skull

(Kapala) The skull represents the cycle of life and death. It is found in all sorts of forms and is depicted with gods who are emphasizing the transient nature of all things, usually when they appear in their terrifying aspect. Thus Durga, and sometimes Shiva, wear a chain of skulls (**kapalamala**) Ganesha, as Heruka, has a garland of five skulls (**panchakapala**) on his head; skull bowls (**kapala**) are depicted in the hands of terrifying gods and the staff or club of a yogi is often decorated with a skull. This club itself is often made of a human bone.

Snake
(Naga) The snake is the symbol of the eternal cycle of time and immortality; in Southern India it is also a symbol of fertility. Most snakes that are depicted are *cobras*. Three, five or seven-headed snakes in illustrations often serve as a protective canopy behind a god's head.

Spear
(Shula) This is the weapon of Skanda and Agni. Traditionally the spear was made to be an invincible weapon of Vishvakarma, the creator of the universe.

Spoon
(Sruk) The spoon is used to pour clarified butter (ghee) in the sacrificial fire. Therefore, in the hand of a god, it shows that a god can also make sacrifices. This attribute is particularly depicted with Brahma, Sarasvati and Agni, as well as Annapurna, the generous manifestation of Parvati.

Staff

(Danda) This serves in particular as a punishment for offences against the universal law of time. In its earliest form it was a bone, and at a later stage it was topped by a skull; eventually the skull remained the only ornamentation. The staff is carried by gods in their terrifying and destructive manifestations.

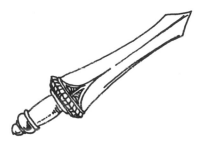

Sword

(Khadga) This is the symbol of wisdom, the battle against ignorance and the force of destruction. It is an object of reverence which brings good luck or bad luck, depending on its size.

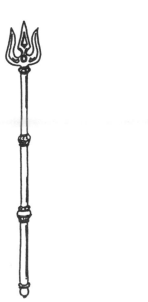

Trident

(Trishula) In Northern India, Shiva is always depicted with the attributes of a trident and a cobra; in Southern India, with the antelope and the battle axe. The three prongs of the trident represent the three aspects of the god as Creator, Protector and Destroyer. When the shaft is long this symbolizes the axis of the universe. Like the bolt of lightening the trident is honoured as a magic means of driving out demons.

Vase

(Kalasha) This is the symbol of abundance, wisdom and immortality. It contains the nectar of eternal life (amrita). It is the attribute of Brahma, Shiva as a teacher, and Lakshmi. Also see: *water jug.*

Watering-can

(Kamandalu) Water has always been a symbol of life fertility, and therefore wealth. While the vase serves to catch the nectar of eternal life, the watering-can serves to pour it out again. It is above all, gods who appear in the form of a beggar, ascetic or holy man who have the watering-can as an attribute (Brahma, Shiva and the water gods, Varuna, Ganga and Sarasvati).

Wheel

(Chakra) Originally the sun wheel, this became the symbol of the cycle of life and death. It is often depicted as a wheel with spokes, but also as a disc or sun. In this form it is also considered to be a weapon. It is particularly found as an attribute of Vishnu and Surya.

Yoni

Female sexual organ, symbol of fertility, (See: lingam)

Part 4

Animals

Animal Gods and Divine Animals

Just as in the life of man, animals also play an important role for the gods. Traces of a totemic past, and symbols of fertility are reflected in the uses of animals and in illustrations. However, the paradoxical nature of the gods themselves, in whom greatly conflicting characteristics are united without difficulty, can also be identified in the symbolism of animals.

So far, three animals have already been mentioned: the antelope, the snake and the mongoose. These are used as attributes in an almost abstract symbolic sense. However, animals are also very common in a more direct way, e.g., as a form of transport. Almost every god has his own animal to ride, and he/she is often depicted with this animal. Sometimes the animal carries the god on its back, and sometimes it supports the throne on which the god is seated (see photograph, p. 56). Other animals are also found in the illustrations. These refer to a particular aspect of the god or to a special legend.

Animals also appear as independent divine creatures in some illustrations. In some cases, a god may partly or wholly assume the form of an animal, such as Vishnu, in a number of his incarnations.

The animals which particular gods ride are mentioned here, but are usually illustrated with the particular god concerned.

Lakshmi-Narayana with Garunda

Animal Gods

A number of animals have the status of a god or demi-god. Of these, Ganesha, the god with an elephant's head, plays a role which is not comparable with that of other gods. He is one of the greatest and most popular Hindu gods (see Part 7).

The snake

From ancient times up to the present, snakes (**nagas**) have been honoured in India. They are the patron saints of waterways, lakes and springs, and therefore a symbol of life and fertility. As they appear to constantly regenerate themselves by shedding their skin, they are also a symbol of the eternal cycle of time and immortality.

Nagas are viewed as semi-divine, semi-demonic creatures, and are represented either in the form of a cobra, or as a creature which is half animal or half fair youth. They are all descendants of the snake kings, Vasuki, Takshaka and Shesha. They inhabit the water paradises and guard all the treasures of the earth. They are cunning, wise, potent and supernaturally strong. Above all, they are dangerous: as guardians of sources of water, their friendship must be secured by sacrifices. In mythical tales, snake kings play a special role. The world is supported by the head of **Vasuki**, and when he shakes himself, he causes earthquakes. When the ocean of milk was churned (see part 7), Vasuki was available as a cord ?? to turn the mountain Mandara, which served as the beater to churn the milk.

Vishnu rests in a cosmic slumber in the coils of the snake, Shesha (also see Part 7).

The monkey

As an inhabitant of the woods (Vanara), the monkey has traditionally been seen as the divine protector of the country people of Southern India who cultivated their fields in the jungle and were also known as Vanaras themselves.

In the Ramayana (see Part 6), the hero, Rama, secures the aid of the armies of the divine king of the monkeys, **Sugriva**, who is sometimes viewed as the son of the sun god, Surya. These armies of monkeys are characterized by their incomparable courage and strength. Their leader, **Hanuman**, has in particular achieved immortality, both literally and metaphorically, by his impressive feats of courage, supernatural strength and devotion.

Venaras are usually depicted as men with the head of a monkey and a tail, often in a pose of submission and quiet obedience (holding one hand in front of the mouth).

The birdman

The demigod, **Garuda**, who is part man and part eagle, is best known as the creature which carries Vishnu (see Part 7 and p. 56). He is the king of the birds, a symbol of the wind and the sun, and equally fast. The unimaginable speed with which he travels from one world to another effortlessly, means that he is also a symbol of the esoteric wisdom of the Vedas. The power of the magical words of these writings can give man symbolic wings with which he too can move from one world to the next with the speed of light or of Garuda.

Holy animals

One of the most common stereotypes which prevails in the west about
Hinduism in India is that "sacred cows walk in the streets". It is true
that the cow is a sacred animal, symbolically viewed as the Holy
Feeder, and it may not be killed under any circumstances.

The mythical original mother of all cows, a symbol of abundance, is
Surabhi. Her excrement is sacred, and she grants purity, heath and
prosperity.

When a person dies, he must cross a river to the underworld. He is
helped by cows who protect him against the man eating crocodiles in
the river, so that he can have a new existence.

The **bull** is the symbol of male reproductive power. Its four legs
represent truth, purity, compassion and generosity. Touching a bull's
tail is said to liberate man from any impurity. The white bull belongs
with Shiva as an emblem and as the creature which he rides (see Part
7), while the black bull goes with Yama (see Part 5).

Animals of carriage

In addition to the animals mentioned above, we include a summary of a number of animals which specific gods ride, so that the god concerned can immediately be recognized from the animal. Some animals are also depicted as independent elements. In this case, they serve as an emblem, and their main significance is shown in the list below.

Antelope	–	nature, king of the animals	–	**Vaya, Soma**
Goose	–	breath of life, boundlessness	–	**Brahma, Sarasvati**
Dog	–	impurity, guardian of hell	–	**Bhairava, Rudra**
Lion	–	strength, protection	–	**Durga, Parvati**
Elephant	–	strength, equanimity, wealth	–	**Indra**
Horse	–	courage	–	**Indra, Surya**
Parrot	–	immortality, love	–	**Kama, goddesses**
Peacock	–	immortality	–	**Skanda**
Ram/ billygoat	–	force of earthly fire	–	**Agni**
Tiger	–	power of destruction	–	**Kali**
Sea monster	–	fertility in water	–	**Ganga, Varuna**

Part 5

The Vedic Gods

From Natural Phenomenon to Human God

All over the world, religion started in the form of an animistic natural religion: all natural phenomena which exercised a great but unexplained influence acquired their own personality which could be invoked and appealed to, though this was not a human personality.

The people of the Indus valley probably also viewed natural phenomena as divine entities. These entities did not yet have any human form: the wind, sun, mountains, trees, water, earth, fire, and sky were still worshipped in their original form, particularly with sacrificial fires.

This slowly changed with the arrival of the Indo-Aryans: gradually the divine natural phenomena assumed animal, and later human forms. Probably the earliest Vedic gods did not yet have any tangible form, but were reflected in representations. The effigies of these divine creatures or natural forces tended to be made in the spirit of the people who sought an identifiable form for the object of their devotion. In the later Vedas they became very human creatures with human characteristics and desires. the early books mention three gods; later there are thirty-three, and later still it is said that three hundred, three thousand and thirty-nine gods worshipped Agni.

At first, all these gods had equal powers, and were so like humans that they were mortal. Finally, a number of them acquired immortality by making sacrifices, and Agni, Indra and Surya became superior to other gods. Together they formed a divine trinity which was later replaced (or repelled) by other trinities.

There are so many different stories about the origins of the gods that many interpretations are possible. Prajapati, the Creator, is sometimes called the Father of all gods, while in other places in the Vedas this is Indra. However, Dyaus (Heaven) and Prithivi (Earth), who are among the oldest known gods, are also referred to as the parents of all other gods, and sometimes it is considered that the god Soma was created by the other gods, while at other times he is mentioned as the Creator of the gods. Thus, even at that time the god of the moment is the most important at that particular time, and the source of everything else, including other gods.

Apart from such individual preferences, the god **Agni** can perhaps be identified as one of the first gods to acquire a human form. Even in pre-Vedic times the sacrificial fire was an important religious practice, and this survived into the Vedic period with its many sacrificial rituals. This sacrificial fire was embodied in Agni, who lived among mortals as an immortal god and served as a messenger between man and the gods by carrying the sacrifices to heaven. Agni is depicted with two or seven arms, two heads and three legs. In each head he has seven fiery tongues with which he licks up the sacrificial butter. He rides a ram or in a chariot harnessed with fiery horses. His attributes are an axe, torch, prayer beads and flaming spear, although he is also depicted with other attributes.

Surya, the sun god, is also mentioned as the creator of the universe, and his children, Yama and Yami, were supposedly the first human beings. For centuries, Surya, who was also known as Savita, was worshipped in temples specially devoted to him. Eventually Vishnu took over this predominant position. In modern Hinduism he holds a modest position between the other gods who are associated with the planets and celestial bodies. Surya drives through heaven in a triumphal chariot, harnessed with seven horses or one horse with seven heads. The charioteer is **Arjuna**, the god of sunrise. Sometimes Surya has two hands with a lotus in each hand, sometimes four, with a lotus, wheel and conch shell; in this case, the fourth hand makes a gesture of protection.

Indra, the god of the natural elements, was the king of all the gods to whom most of the Vedic hymns are dedicated. When the earth dried up, he was offered the intoxicating soma plant. While he was under the influence of this plant, Indra fought against the demon drought and expelled him with his weapons, thunder and lightning. It started to rain, and Indra saved the earth and its inhabitants.

Indra rides the royal elephant, which is often depicted with three trunks and/or four tusks. He has four arms and his attributes can include a bolt of lightning, lance, sword, bow and arrow, net and conch shell. He also makes the gestures of protection and wish fulfilment. Sometimes Indra is depicted with two arms, and eyes all over his body. In the course of time his position weakened and he was king only of the lesser gods and the lord of heaven (Svarga) where the gods dwell.

Soma was originally the god of ecstasy, the Indian Dionysus. His nectar, **amrita**, is the food of the gods, There is also an intoxicating beverage which was made from the legendary soma plant, though it is still unclear exactly which plant this was.

Later, Soma also became the god of the moon. This meant he was the son of Varuna, the lord of the oceans, from which the moon rises. During half of the month, 36,000 gods feed on Soma's nectar to retain their immortality. Soma becomes so exhausted that he wastes away (the waning moon). Then Surya feeds him with the water of the oceans, Soma regains his strength and the moon grows full again.

Soma, who is also known as Chandra, rides in a chariot drawn by ten white horses or by an antelope.

Varuna was originally the lord of the cosmic order. The sun was his eye, the wind his breath. Soma was his son. Following a battle between gods and demons, the gods decided to establish a clearer order of importance, and Varuna was left only as the god of the oceans. Varuna's most important attribute is the lasso. He is depicted with two or four arms and he rides on **Makara**, a sea monster which is half-fish and half-antelope.

Vayu is the god of the wind. He is also known as Vata or Pavan (the purifier). He is described in the hymns as having "exceptional beauty", and he moves on noisily in his shining coach. This is drawn by white or purple horses, sometimes two, sometimes forty-nine, sometimes even a thousand. His main attribute is a white banner.

Yama was originally the first mortal. When he had found the way to the other world by dying, he accompanied those who died after him. In this way he became king of the invisible world, and finally the judgemental god of death. In illustrations his skin is green, his garments are red, and he wears a golden throne and a flower in his hair. He has a club in one of his two or four hands and he rides a black buffalo or bull.

Vishvakarma, also known as Tvastri, is the creator of the gods. He made all the weapons and triumphal chariots used by the gods, the creator of the universe and everything in it and is thus the protector of all living things. He is also the god of craftsmen. He is usually depicted with four hands and is surrounded by numerous tools. Additional attributes include a water jug, a lasso, a book, and sometimes a club.

Kubera is mentioned in the Vedas as the prince of demons and spirits which live in the shadows. Later he was viewed as the lord of the yakshas, the earthly spirits, who is the guardian of all the treasures on earth. Together with the gods Indra, Varuna and Yama, he was one of the Digpalas, the Guards of the Points of the Compass.

Kuberta became the god of wealth and abundance only at a much later stage. There is one story which relates how Kubera had been a thief in a previous life and had broken into one of Shiva's temples. The light went out and the persistence with which Kubera tried to bring back the light into the sacred temple moved Shiva so much that he gave the thief the immortal status of a god in his next life. Another version relates how Kubera spent thousands of years as a strict ascetic, which impressed the god Brahma so much that he made Kubera the god of wealth. Kubera is depicted with a fat belly as a sign of wealth. His main attribute is a mongoose, as well as a club, a pomegranate, a water jug and a money pouch.

Part 6

The Epic Period

Acseticism and Devotion

The Indo-Aryans gradually lost their nomadic character; they settled mainly in the plains of Northern India, where they built their cities. The various different cultures in India started to intermingle. The ritual sacrifice lost its significance, and the doctrine of the Upanishads with the concepts of Brahman and Atman gained ground. It was only during this period that concepts such as karma and reincarnation were introduced. The young prince, Siddharta, sought salvation from the wheel of rebirth and achieved Buddhahood; his teachings undoubtedly arose from the philosophies which were introduced at that time about rebirth and salvation, but in their turn they had an unmistakable influence on the continued development of Hinduism.

In the course of the following centuries, two great literary works were written, the **Ramayana** and the **Mahabharata**, which combined historical events with philosophical, religious and social aspects. In fact, both works are a series of heroic epics about royal children who became ensnared in the dilemma of choosing between a life which maintains the world order and a life which withdraws from this world in the quest for individual liberation. The world famous **Bhagavad Gita** (The Song of God), part of the Mahabharata, gives a possible solution for this inner conflict; it is not necessary to withdraw from the world to achieve true detachment – true detachment lies in disinterested action which is carried out only for the act itself and not with a view to the ultimate result.

While these heroic epics are, on the one hand, a result of and an inspiration for a new way of thinking which arose at this time, they also have a great influence on the experience of the divine world. The human heroes in the stories constantly came across gods who not only help them, but also challenge them, set tasks and teach lessons. Some of these humans eventually become gods themselves. Because of the wealth of stories in which the gods in their turn act so clearly, and often in a very human way, the way in which these gods are viewed is also more detailed and vibrant. History, religion, philosophy, and mythology are interwoven in a way unparalleled in world literature. An extensive school of religious practice is based on this, as well as an entire social system. The caste system which is explained in the Dharma Shastras (Books of the Law), written at roughly the same time, is, for example, clearly illustrated in the Mahabharata in the experiences and views of the protagonists, the Pandavas and the Kauravas, two groups of cousins who fight each other.

Vyasa, the wise one, dictates the Mahabharata to Ganesha

The Mahabharata is a very detailed account of the rise and fall of the Kuru dynasty.

The god, Vishnu, had already appeared in the Rig-Veda. He is described in detail in Part 7 of the Puranas. There are twelve known incarnations of Vishnu, forms in which he came down to earth in order to restore order in difficult times. It was during the Epic period that he assumed a clearly human form to influence the course of events. In the Mahabharata he appears in his eighth incarnation as Krishna.

After wandering for a long time, Prince Krishna of the Yadava clan came to the most western part of India, Gujarat, where he made friends with the Pandavas, the five sons of King Pandu, and his wives, Kunti and Madri, though the sons were actually begotten by five other gods. He was their counsellor and ally, for example, in the battle against King Jarasandha in Magadh.

When the battle for supremacy which had raged ever since their birth between the Pandavas and their hundred cousins, the Kauravas, finally led to war, both parties asked Krishna to help in the battle. As the Pandavas saw him first, they were able to choose first. They could either have Krishna's large army on their side, or Krishna himself, though he would not fight with them. The Pandavas wished above all to have Krishna himself on their side. He would only drive the chariot of Arjuna, the unparalleled archer, and give advice. The Kauravas were satisfied with the large army.

However, during the battle, Krishna was cursed by the entire Kaurava clan for the advice which he gave the Pandavas, and which in some cases directly contravened the code of honour of the warrior caste, the Kshatryas.

The battle was won by the Pandavas, who stood for just principles and righteous action. Krishna crowned the oldest, Yudhisthira, king. However, because of the curse of the Kauravas, Krishna's own clan was completely wiped out, and he himself died as he lay asleep, and a hunter who mistook his fair feet for a deer, shot him dead by mistake.

The Bhagavad Gita

As stated in Part 1, the principle of Brahman (impersonal Divine Power) was introduced in the Vedic period. The human soul (Atman), which is part of Brahman, is hindered from becoming united with Brahman by the illusion of worldly matters. By refraining from being active in the world (asceticism), it is possible to achieve a reunification.

Another way of becoming united with the Divine is that of reverence, devotion and surrender to a personal god (Bhakti). This personal form of love between god and man first appeared in Hinduism in about 200 BC in the Bhagavad Gita, part of the Mahabharata.

When the fight for the throne between the Pandavas and the Kauravas reached a dramatic climax at the battle of Kurukshetra and all the warriors on each side were standing ready in their chariots, the great warrior of the Pandavas, **Arjuna**, was filled with doubt about whether what he was about to do was right. There would be so many victims on each side – was it really worth it? He discussed this crisis of conscience with his friend and charioteer, **Krishna**, the incarnation of the highest one (the eighth incarnation of Vishnu). Krishna's answer was a lesson in moral values, social conduct and human ethics, and it entered world literature as "the Song of God" (Bhagavad Gita). In this respect it is striking that the noble ideas about spiritual detachment and pure thought with which Krishna presented Arjuna are very different from the sometimes rather sly conduct characterized by the motto, "the end justifies the means", which he put forward in other places in the Mahabharata. Later on, when Krishna wandered over the world as a cowherd, and had love affairs with you girls tending the cows, this aspect of the detached counsellor did not reappear.

In the myth itself, the "author" of the Mahabharata, of which the Bhagavad Gita forms part, is the wise Vyasa, who dictated the whole saga to the elephant god, Ganesha. According to other versions, the Bhagavad Gita was the result of a religion, Bhagvat, which was preached by a certain Vasudeva Krishna.

It was only eight centuries after the Bhagavad Gita that the practice of Bhakti became a general religious practice spreading from the south of India. The Nayanars, followers of Shiva, and the Alvars, followers of Vishnu, surrendered to a form of joyful ecstatic devotion which has played an increasingly important role in Hindu religious practice ever since that time.

Krishna and Arjuna on the battlefield of Kurukshetra

The Ramayama

The entire epic of **Ramayama** is devoted to the seventh incarnation of Vishnu, the hero, Rama.

From a purely historical point of view, the Ramayama is the story of the development of the Aryan people as they became a well-armed, strategically strong nation which gradually moved to the south and conquered the people who lived there. From a mythical point of view, the Ramayama is a story of heroism, brotherly love and devoted marriage.

Vishnu decided to descend to earth in order to slay the king of the demons, Ravana. As Rama, son of king Dasharatha, he won the hand of Sita, the foster daughter of King Janaka. Dasharatha wished to appoint Rama as regent, but one of his wives reminded him of his promise to crown her son as king, and Rama was banished. He fled to the woods together with Sita and his half-brother, Lakshmana. When they were there, Sita was abducted by the king of the demons. Rama and Lakshmama went in search of her. On their way, they helped the monkey king, Sugriva, to fight an opponent, and were rewarded with an army of monkeys led by Hanuman. When Hanuman succeeded in finding Sita on the island of Lanka (now known as Sri Lanka), the monkeys built a bridge from the mainland to the island and there was a terrible battle between Rama and the army of demons. In the end, Rama won the battle and was able to take his wife back home.

However, before taking Sita into his arms, Rama wanted to test her loyalty. He accused her of being unfaithful to him while she was in captivity. Sita felt deeply wounded and threw herself into the fire to prove that she had been chaste. When the god of fire, Agni, did not harm her in any way, and placed her in Rama's arms untouched, Rama finally believed in his wife's fidelity.

Unfortunately, Rama later once again believed rumours about Sita's infidelity, and rejected her, even though she was pregnant. When he realized much later from Sita's two sons that he had been mistaken, and showed his regret, it was too late. Sita no longer wished to live with Rama. She asked the goddess of the earth to take her into her lap. The earth opened up, and Sita, who has always been seen by the people as the goddess who protects the fields, disappeared forever.

Rama and Sita

Hanuman, who was originally only a minister in the Ramayana, and then became a leader in battle, made such an impression with his unceasing devotion and loyalty that he has been revered as a god ever since. He is usually depicted with the head of a monkey and a muscular human body. He carries a large club in his hand.

One very popular representation of Hanuman shows him flying, holding a mountain landscape in one hand. During the great battle between Rama and Ravana, Hanuman flew to the mountain Mahudaya in the Himalayas to fetch healing herbs for the deadly wounded Lakshmana. As he was not sure exactly which herbs it was best to pick, he decided to take the entire mountain on which the herbs grew so that Lakshmana's doctor could choose for himself.

Part 7

The Puranic Gods

Regrouping and integration

Following the great epic works, a number of long narrative works were written. These are the Puranas, which have influenced all of Hindu religion from the time it started, up to now.

The Puranas can be roughly divided into three groups of stories; each group of stories is based on one god, and the spouses, incarnations, manifestations, any children they have, and gods who accompany them. These three gods, who are still seen and worshipped as the Great Trinity, Trimurti, are **Brahma**, **Vishnu**, and **Shiva**.

In principle, these gods are equal in power and influence, as they are actually no more than the reflection of the three aspects (creation, preservation and destruction) of the One Divine Power. In the classic representation of Trimurti this is how they are depicted: as three heads on one neck, and often even three faces on one head, each looking in a different direction. For the observer, Brahma, the creator, looks to the left, Vishnu, the preserver, looks straight ahead, and Shiva, the destroyer, looks to the right (see photograph, p. 82).

However, in the part of the Puranas devoted to a particular god, this god is described as the only great god who is superior to all other gods. For example, the part of the Puranas which is devoted to Vishnu always describes Vishnu as the victor in the battle between him and Shiva; the part of the Puranas devoted to Shiva obviously always describes this god as being victorious in the same battle.

Trimurti, part of a wooden temple cart, Southern India

Many elements from the Puranas, including some gods, date back to the period before the arrival of the Aryans. In Southern India particularly, there was a strong belief in local gods and goddesses; divine qualities were attributed to trees, rivers and mountains, as well as to animals, rather as they were in the valley of the Indus. As Hinduism spread further south, more and more of these divine figures and forces were incorporated in the already richly populated pantheon. In the Puranas, all these gods and the stories told about them were given a place.

The most ideal form in which a Purana can be written deals with five main subjects. The Vishnu Purana, which is closest to this ideal, is subdivided as follows:

1. The creation of the universe;
2. The destruction and recreation of the universe;
3. The line of descent from gods and patriarchs;
4. The dominance of the Manus, the fourteen mythological ancestors of man who each ruled over the earth for a period of 4,320,000 years;
5. The history of the two great royal houses of the sun and the moon.

Not only were many gods from before the Vedic period, as well as Vedic gods of less significance, included in the Puranas; in many cases a number of them were also combined to become a single important god. Sometimes a number of these gods, and even popular heroes, were recreated as different forms (of Shiva) and avatars, i.e., incarnations on earth (of Vishnu). Vishnu is a good example of this process. In the Vedas he was a subordinate god. During the Epic period, he was identified with the hero Krishna, who thus changed from a man with some divine qualities to a god in human form. In the Puranas, this Krishna is combined with a shepherd god who plays the flute; his character changed slightly, and he became the subject of many poems and legends and is still the object of devout worship today.

This was the period when the great temples were built, and stories about these "dwellings of the gods" were told, showing the importance of a particular place above all other places. Anonymous artists started to sculpt in stone the "language of the gods", their manifestations, and their legendary deeds and powers.

Brahma riding his goose

Brahma

In the Upanishads, Brahman was the all-pervading Divine Essence: everything flowed from this and everything returned to it. This Essence did not have any form, but was present in everything. Later, many legends were told about the birth of Brahma as a personified god. One of these legends relates that the formless lord of the universe, who existed in himself, created the waters of the earth and planted a seed from which a golden egg developed. He was hatched from this egg in the form of Brahma, the Absolute creator of the universe.

In Hindu cosmology, the time of creation is recorded in the days and years of the life of Brahma. When Brahma awoke from his sleep and opened his eyes, a universe and everything in it was created. When he shuts his eyes at the end of the day to go to sleep, that universe comes to an end. One day in the life of Brahma is known as Kalpa, and lasts 4,320 million human years. One year in Brahma's life lasts 360 of these days and nights. Brahma's life lasts 100 of these years ...

Probably the rather abstract character of Brahma was responsible for the fact that he gradually moved further into the background, and that there are now only a few temples left which are devoted to him. Brahma has four faces, of which only three are visible. That is how he is usually depicted: with three faces and four hands. The four faces represent the four Vedas, and the four hands represent the points of the compass. His face is red or pink. He is represented either standing up or sitting on a lotus, or riding his goose, the symbol of knowledge. Sometimes he rides in a coach drawn by seven geese, symbolizing the seven worlds. Often he is dressed in a tiger skin or in a black antelope skin. The attributes which are depicted with him include a water jug, the symbol of his function as the creator (all life springs forth from water), a spoon, a sceptre, his bow Parivita, a book (the Vedas), a lotus and prayer beads, of which the beads represent time.

Sarasvati is sometimes described as the wife, and sometimes as the daughter of Brahma. Originally she was a goddess of the rivers and of fertility, and in this role she was Vishnu's wife. Later he gave her to Brahma, and she became the goddess of knowledge, poetry and music. She is described as a great beauty with a milky white face, dressed in white garments. Standing or sitting on a water lily, or riding a goose, she plays the vina (Indian lute). In the other two of her four hands she holds a book (the Vedas), and prayer beads. Other manifestations of Sarasvati include Brahmi or Bramani, with four heads, four hands, a trident and prayer beads, and Vagadevi or Vigishvari, the goddess of speech.

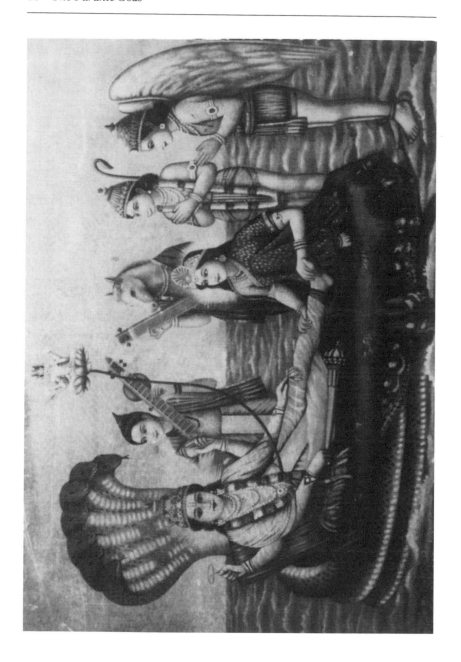

Vishnu Narayana, floating on Sheshanaga

Vishnu

The Padma Purana describes how the Higher Being wished to create the world. To do this he created himself from his own left side in the form of Brahma. In order to maintain what he had created, he brought forth Vishnu from his right side, and in order to be able to destroy everything, he created Shiva from the centre of his body.

The illustrations, as well as the floating sculptures of **Vishnu Narayana** are well known. He sleeps soundly in the coils of the snake Shesha, with his wife Lakshmi at his feet (see illustration). The snake floats on the infinite cosmic ocean. In his sleep, Vishnu watches everything being created, and as a result a lotus flower blooms in his navel. When the flower opens, Brahma appears seated inside it to live out his life of a hundred Brahma years, which were described above. After this period, Vishnu stops dreaming, the lotus flower closes again and withdraws, and is then recreated in the next dream, and so on ...

Vishnu is usually depicted with a black or blue complexion. He has four arms and is clad in yellow. He wears a high crown, and the sacrificial cord is wound around his torso. His attributes include a club, chakra, conch shell and lotus flower. The heads of Shesha are entwined above his head like a protective canopy. As the king of his own paradise, Vaikuntha, he is known as **Vaikunthanatha**, and is depicted with four heads and eight arms.

In the Rig-Veda, Vishnu is a subordinate god, a manifestation of the energy of the sun. In the Vedas, he is sometimes associated with Indra. Here he is not yet the important god he becomes later, but is already described as the "invincible protector", a title which refers to his future function of preserver of the universe.

It was only in the Mahabharata that Vishnu became the second god in

the great trinity, and gradually embodied the qualities of goodness
and mercy, an aspect in which he is still revered on a large scale today.

Lakshmi, the goddess of wealth and happiness, is Vishnu's wife.
When she is depicted separately, she has four hands: in two of them
she is holding lotus flowers, while the other two bestow the gifts of
well-being and prosperity. When she is depicted with Vishnu,
Lakshmi has only two hands. Usually she has a golden colour. She sits
or stands on a lotus flower, and sometimes has elephants on either
side.
Lakshmi is one of the most popular goddesses. She is also associated
with beauty, and like Sita, Rama's wife, she is associated with farm-
ing.

Kama, the god of love, who was known in Vedic times, and is also known as Yaksha, the spirit of nature, is Vishnu's son, according to later interpretations. He has a bow made of flowers with five arrows (the five senses), with which he inspires lovers, and rides a parrot, the symbol of sensuality.

Vishnu rides **Garuda**, a creature which is half-bird, half-man, usually depicted as a man, sometimes with wings, and often with a beak instead of a nose. Occasionally he appears as a bird. He is the king of the birds, the symbol of wind and sun, and moves from one world to the other with the speed of the wind or of light.

The Ten Incarnations of Vishnu

Over the centuries many gods have been identified with Vishnu in the form of animals and humans. These figures did not acquire the character of a manifestation, but of an incarnation. Whenever the world was in danger because the forces of evil threatened to overcome goodness, Vishnu descended from his heaven to be incarnated on earth. There are ten main incarnations (**avatars**) which have appeared, and will still appear on earth in successive periods. They are related to the developmental stages of human evolution. In addition, there are fourteen subsidiary incarnations.

The first incarnation is that of **Matsya**, the fish-man.
Manu, the ancestor of mankind, was ordered by a fish to build a boat because there was to be a great flood. When the flood came, this ark was pulled along by a large fish. There was a pair of every living creature in the ark. The fish also saved the Vedas from the hands of the demon, Hayagriva. Matsya has four arms and the attributes of a wheel, conch shell, club and lotus flower.

Kurma, the tortoise man, is the second incarnation.

In those days, gods and demons were constantly fighting, and in the end the demons became so strong that the gods were in danger of losing their power. Then Vishnu advised them to churn the ocean of milk so that the amrita (the nectar of immortality) would float to the top and make them invincible. The mountain Mandara was used as the dasher to churn the milk, but when it almost disappeared into the ocean bed, Vishnu changed himself into a tortoise so that his hard shell could support the mountain. (For the churning of the ocean of milk, also see under **Shiva**.)

In this incarnation, Vishnu has four arms, and is accompanied by the attributes of a wheel, conch shell, lotus flower and club. The lower half of his body is replaced by a tortoise.

Varaha, the third incarnation, is a man with the head of a wild boar. Sometimes he is depicted simply as an animal.

According to one of the myths of the Flood, which is at the same time the story of a new cycle of creation, a demon had abducted the goddess of the earth, Prithivi, and hidden her at the bottom of the ocean. Vishnu assumed the form of a giant boar, dived down to the ocean bed and fought the demon, finally defeating him. Then he took the earth goddess back to the surface and helped her to become suitable again for carrying living creatures by creating the continents and sculpting mountains.

Sometimes Varaha is depicted with two arms, but usually he is depicted with four, holding the traditional attributes of Vishnu.

Narasimha is half-man, half-lion, and is the fourth incarnation.
A gatekeeper of Vishnu had enraged him and was condemned to live
out the rest of his life as a demon. Brahma granted him a special boon,
which was that he could not be injured by any weapon either by man
or by animal, by day or by night, inside or outside. He became so over-
confident that he started to make the lives of the gods very difficult,
and Vishnu decided to intervene. In the form of a man with the head
of a lion (neither animal nor man), he hid in one of the two pillars at
the entrance to the house of the demon, Hiranyakasipu, grabbed him
at dusk (neither day nor night) on the threshold of his house (neither
inside nor outside) and mauled him with his claws (without weapons).

Vamana, the fifth incarnation, is the first which had a completely human form, although it was that of a dwarf.

The grandson of Hiranyakasipu, Bali, had overpowered the three worlds and banished the gods from heaven. The gods asked Vishnu to help them, and he devised a plan. He approached King Bali in the form of a dwarf and asked him for a place where he could meditate, which he could encircle with three paces. Bali agreed, and immediately the dwarf transformed himself into the giant, Trivikrama. One pace encircled heaven, the second the earth, and when the third step looked as though it would encircle the underworld, Bali gave way and asked Vishnu to stand on his head instead. In this way Vishnu pushed Bali down into the underworld, where he became king.

Vamana is usually depicted with two arms. He often carries a parasol, and sometimes a water jug and/or a book. He has long hair, often tied up in a topknot, and is dressed in a loincloth or antelope skin.

Parashurama, Rama with an axe, is the sixth incarnation. This time Vishnu assumes a completely human form.

The story of Parashurama dates from the time when there was a lengthy struggle between the two highest castes, the caste of the priests or brahmans, and the caste of warriors, the kshatryas. The priest Jamadagnya had a cow which could grant wishes. The king wanted this cow for himself at any price, and had it stolen. In revenge, Parashurama, the son of the priest, killed the king, who was avenged in his turn by his son, who killed the priest. This resulted in a a terrible war between Parashurama, the brahman, and the kshatryas, which finally ended in victory for Parashurama after twenty-one battles. The young brahman is depicted with two or four hands. He wears his hair in a topknot like an ascetic, and always holds a battle axe in one of his hands, as well as possibly a sword and a bow and arrow.

Rama, also known as Ramachandra, is the seventh incarnation. He is depicted as a young king with two arms, often with a bow and arrow, and frequently accompanied by his wife, Sita (an incarnation of Lakshmi) at his side. Rama is the hero of the epic work, the **Ramayana.** He and his wife are still today seen as the symbol of incorruptibility, honesty, loyalty and tenderness. They have become the subject of countless plays, dances, and nowadays even of films and cartoon strips.

Krishna, the eighth incarnation of Vishnu, is considered to be the most important and is worshipped by millions of people as a god in his own right. The name Krishna ("the black one") was already found in the Upanishads. Later on there are detailed stories about the hero Krishna in the Mahabharata. The Puranas, especially the Bhagavata Parana, contain an exhaustive account of Krishna's life described in numerous colourful tales about his exceptional strength.

The mythological explanation of his black skin (often also represented as blue) is that Vishnu plucked two hairs from his head, a white hair and a black hair. These hairs ended up in the wombs of Rohini and Devaki; Krishna's older brother, **Balarama**, was born from the white hair, and Krishna from the black hair.

Vishnu came down to earth to put an end to the tyranny of King Kamsa. When he heard about this, the king captured Krishna's future mother, Devaki, and murdered all her children as soon as they were born. Vishnu intervened, and saved first Balarama, and later Krishna.

Krishna Venugopala

The young Krishna grew up with Nanda and Yashoda amongst the cowherds. There are many illustrations of this child, Bala-Krishna, which are moving because they represent a real child and not a small adult god, as is the case, for example, with regard to Shiva's sons. The stories describe Krishna's exploits as a child, and the miraculous strength which he revealed.

Krishna grew up to become a fair youth, and for a time he liked nothing better than to play with the gopis, the girls who looked after the cows. In the autumn nights he enchanted them with his charming flute playing, and danced with them in the moonlight (Krishna Venugopala).

Radha is the most important of Krishna's many wives. The love between Krishna and Radha, and Radha's devotion to her lover, in time became an allegory for the love between Krishna the god and his followers, as well as of the follower's devotion (bhakti) to the god. In addition, the two-in-one Krishna-Radha, embodies the tantric principle of the two aspects of the divine (make and female), which together form One (for Tantra, see Mahadevi). During his life on earth Krishna defeated many enemies. He slew the above-mentioned King Kamsa and the snake king, Kaliya, but was also victorious in his battles with the Vedic god, Indra, on several occasions. This is probably one of the many indications that the figure of Krishna came from the rural population of Southern India, the dark, (black!) Dravidians. In addition to illustrations of Krishna as a child, he is depicted in many other ways. His skin is almost always blue or black. Often his right leg is crossed in front of his left leg, with his toes lightly supported on the ground, but there are also many illustrations of him as a dancer, e.g., dancing on the many heads of the snake Kaliya after defeating him. He rides on Garuda. Probably the two best known representations are those of Krishna and Arjuna in their chariot, and of Krishna as a youth playing the flute.

Sometimes he is depicted with four arms with the attributes of Vishnu. The Bhakti movement which flourished in the fifteenth century, probably better known in the west as the Hare Krishna movement, resulted in a large number of works of art, particularly paintings, devoted to Krishna.

Buddha is seen in Hinduism as the ninth incarnation of Vishnu. This incarnation dates from the period in which Buddhism gained greater popularity, particularly amongst the lower castes. The ideas of the brahmans (priests), who felt threatened by this, were as follows. At the beginning of the present era, the age of Kali, Vishnu decided to go down to earth again in order to preach a false religion, and in this way separate the true believers, who could not be dissuaded, from the "heretics". According to another interpretation, Vishnu decided to go down to earth to put an end to the arrogance and oppression of the brahmans, and to purify Hinduism from the rituals that had grown out of hand. The new doctrine which he preached as Buddha, and which taught that every man could deliver himself from the wheel of rebirth by means of a correct inner attitude, has also appeared in Hinduism since that time.

Buddha is seated on a lotus pedestal, sunk in calm meditation. He has the characteristic short, curly hair with a topknot, and the long earlobes of every manifestation of Buddha. His simple garment is yellow, and he does not wear any ornaments.

Kalki is the last incarnation, which has not yet appeared on earth. At the end of the present age of Kali, mankind will be shrouded in darkness, moral values will have disappeared, and there will be general confusion and chaos. Then Vishnu will return in the form of Kalki, shining like a comet in the sky, and he will save mankind by restoring Dharma, the law of justice. A new era will begin, a period of purity and peace, and Kalki will return to heaven.

This incarnation is usually represented as Vishnu himself, riding a white horse, together with his usual attributes, though the club is usually replaced by a sword. Sometimes Kalki is also depicted as a god with the head of a horse and four arms.

Shiva Nataraja in the temple in Gankaikondacholapuram

Shiva

Although the name **Shiva** ("the friendly one") is not found in the Rig-Veda, he is one of the oldest gods of India. In excavations in Mohenjo-Daro and Harappa, two cities dating from the period of the Indus civilization between 3000 and 2000 BC, images were found of a seated figure with crossed legs. This is the position of meditation which is still used by yogis nowadays. He has three heads and is surrounded by animals. This nameless god is undoubtedly a precursor of Shiva, the Lord of the Three Worlds, the Prince of Ascetics, and the Protector of the Animal Kingdom.

The first name by which this god is found in the Vedas is **Rudra**. Rudra is above all a violent god, the god of storms and destruction, who is also feared by the other gods, although there were benevolent aspects even at that time. These two aspects, the terrifying and the benevolent aspects, have always been characteristics of Shiva.

In the Ramayana and the Mahabharata he was a mountain god who was suddenly powerful but by no means had the qualities which he acquired later. During the Guptas Dynasty, 320-650 AD, Shiva was at the same time a god of love and a god of destruction. He was the god who destroyed creation after every **Kalpa**, and at the same time he became the great ascetic who preserved the world with his meditation. He was related to aspects of fertility, and his symbol was the lingam, the male reproductive organ and the source of his power.

In the course of the more than twenty centuries in which Shiva has been worshipped in some form or other, he has appeared in a wealth of stories which all describe one aspect of him,. and which are often related to one of his many manifestations. In fact, some of these stories are about local gods who acquired a place in the Hindu pantheon as a manifestation of Shiva. Other stories describe some of the

power struggles between the most important gods (and their followers), or relate the replacement/succession of old gods and forms of
religion by the newer personal god.

His manifestations can be roughly divided into five categories: the
young ascetic; the cosmic dancer; the lord of destruction; the terrible
Bhairava; the benevolent protector and loving husband. The terrifying aspects often have the suffix **Ugra**; the benevolent aspects have
the suffix **Saumya**. Some of the general characteristics of his appearance are that he is scantily clad or completely naked, with his long
hair either fanned out, in a topknot or worn in a crown. He has three
eyes which represent the sun, the moon, and fire. He keeps the third
eye shut, for if he opened it the searing heat would scorch all of
creation. He is usually depicted with one face and two or four arms,
although some manifestations show him with up to eighteen arms.
The attributes reveal whether it is a North Indian manifestation
(trident and cobra) or a South Indian manifestation (battle axe and
antelope).

Shiva-Dakshina-Murti or **Mahayogi** is one of the best known illustrations of Shiva. He is seated on the tops of the Himalayas in deep meditation. His abode there is the sacred mountain Kailash, which is still a place of pilgrimage for thousands of pilgrims. The god is represented wearing a simple loincloth, sometimes with the hide of an antelope around him, and seated on a tiger skin, or sometimes on a lotus throne. He wears a moon sickle in his hair and snakes coil around his neck. In his hands he holds a trident and a drum, and his attributes also include a water jug. His face is turned to the south (dakshina), the direction which brings luck. He is the greatest of all the yogis included in the Brahman. He is also the great teacher who reveals to gods and holy men the essence of the sacred texts, and the lord of music. In this function he is also represented separately as **Vinadhara-Murti**, standing or sitting with a lute (vina).

Shiva Natajara

The above-mentioned attributes are related to a story about Shiva and 10,000 rishis (ascetics) who were jealous of the handsome god because all their wives had fallen in love with him. The rishis sent a wild tiger and then an antelope to Shiva, but Shiva killed and skinned them with his bare hands. Then they sent poisonous snakes which he tamed and wore around his neck, and then he caught the red hot iron which the rishis threw at him, and made a weapon with it. When a moon sickle was hurled at his head, he wore this as an ornament in his hair. The ascetics then sent a malevolent black dwarf to him (**Apasmara**), but Shiva knocked him over and then danced on the dwarf's belly. In the end, all the rishis knelt down and worshipped him.

The cosmic dance of Shiva as king of the dance (**Nataraja**) is seen as the symbol of the eternal movement of the universe. The universe was set in motion by the regular rhythm of the dance, and started to manifest itself in all its forms. The gods, demons, and other supernatural creatures surrounded Shiva and looked on in wonder. Sometimes he stops the sound of his drum to look for a new and better rhythm. At that moment the universe ends, to be recreated when the music recommences. The circle of flames around Shiva is energy in its purest form, but also the fire of cremation. At the same time it is the symbol of the holy mantra, AUM, the basic sound of creation. The dwarf under Shiva's foot represents ignorance. The drum in his hand symbolizes the combination of the male and female aspects. The sound of the drum indicates that sound is the source of creation, and god is the source of sound (Nada-Brahman). The fire in the palm of his hand reveals his ability to destroy the universe, and his hand put out in the gesture of an elephant, represents his strength, while his raised foot represents liberation (see photograph).

The dancing Shiva is also depicted in other positions. As **Lalatatilakam**, he has eight or sixteen arms. One leg dances on the dwarf Apasmara, while the other is stretched straight up. As **Tandava**, he is depicted with ten arms, dancing in ecstasy on places where bodies are cremated, accompanied by his goddess, Devi, and a host of spirits.

In many cases a woman's face can be seen in Shiva's hair. This is the river goddess, **Ganga**.

In order to liberate the souls of the 60,000 sons of King Sagar who were burned in the underworld, he begged the goddess Ganga to flow over their ashes. To do this she had to flow from heaven across the earth to the underworld. This was not a simple matter, because the force with which the water would fall on the earth would be too great. Therefore Shiva, who sat on the holy mountain Kailash, spread out his long hair to break the fall. Ganga was furious about this interference, but Shiva captured her in his hair, until she finished raging, and flowed down to the underworld over his head in a placid stream, so that the 60,000 souls could go up to heaven.

Another version of this legend relates how the earth was so dry that there was a great famine. The rishis from the Himalayas begged the river goddess Ganga to descend and make the land fertile once again. But if she were to flow down in one, the dried out land would all be washed away, and therefore ... etc.

These two legends both contain identifiable geographical, as well as ritual elements; the source of the Ganges is at Mount Kailash, Shiva's dwelling place; unfortunately, periods of great drought, followed by flooding, are not unusual in this area. In the course of his development from a mountain god to a husband, Shiva descended from the Himalayas and settled in the city of Benares on the Ganges. Every pilgrim knows the blessing for the eternal soul to die in Benares, preferably on the banks of the Ganges, and to be crenated there so that the ashes can be scattered in the waters of the holy river.

Shiva is depicted standing with four arms as **Gangadhara-Murti**. One hand is lifting up his hair, with an image of the goddess, Ganga, in the hair. Often he is depicted with his wife, Parvati; she is standing next to Shiva, one of his arms is round her as she looks up to Ganga.? It is said that she is jealous, and perhaps she has cause to be; Shiva is often depicted with an erect penis to indicate that he is not entirely unsusceptible to the beauty of the river goddess in his hair.

Shiva's neck is blue. When the god started to churn the ocean of milk (also see under Vishnu), in order to acquire the nectar of immortality, all the creatures on earth appeared from the ocean. In the end the nectar floated to the top, together with the terrible poison, kalakuta, which threatened to destroy the cosmos. Shiva quickly stepped forward and slurped up all the poison so that it could do no more damage, except that it coloured his throat blue forever.

In Shiva's aspect of destroyer, he is the force which maintains the cycle of destruction and creation. He is the great liberator who breaks down everything, thus releasing energy for new growth. He is death which contains life. There are a number of known manifestations, three of which are described below. The suffix *murti* indicates that it is a manifestation which is often linked to a legend about the origin of that manifestation.

As **Gajasura-Murti** he is depicted dancing on the head of an elephant demon. This demon was disrupting the ritual of a number of brahmans who were worshipping Shiva's lingam. Shiva stepped forward from the lingam, chopped off the demon's head, and wrapped the demon's skin around him like a cloak.

In the form of **Tripurantaka-Murti**, Shiva is the hero who was the only one able to destroy the three cities of the Asuras when these demons had gained too much power. No god was able to defeat them, and only Shiva, with the help of the other gods, succeeded in destroying them. This manifestation can be identified by the stance of an archer and the attributes of a bow and arrow.

There are several stories about Shiva defeating the god of death, **Yama**, also known as **Kala**. In many cases this involves a man who is engaged in the worship of Shiva's lingam at the moment that Yama wishes to come for him. Enraged about the interruption of this meditation, Shiva leaps forth from the lingam to repel Yama.

Shiva gave a son to a childless rishi, though he was to die at the age of sixteen. On his sixteenth birthday, this Markandeya was just completing the sacred lingam ritual when Yama came for him. Enraged about this interruption, Shiva sprang forth from the lingam, chased Yama away and granted Markandeya eternal life. In illustrations of this aspect of Shiva, **Kalari-Murti**, he appears jumping from the lingam and raising his foot to kick Yama in the chest.

Probably the best known terrifying manifestation of Shiva is that of
Bhairava, "the Terrible One", who has 64 manifestations. He can be
identified by the hair surrounding his head like flames, and the dog
accompanying him. He wanders round naked, covered only in ashes.
This manifestation is sometime explained by the following story.

The god Brahma desired his own daughter. He was so obsessed by her
that he gave himself a countenance facing each direction, so that he
could watch her wherever she went. The daughter fled to heaven and
Brahma made himself a fifth face, so that he could watch her there as
well. This made Shiva so furious that he appeared as Bhairava and
chopped off Brahma's fifth head. In punishment for this sin, Bhairava
was forced to wander through the universe, begging and half-mad
with remorse, holding Brahma's skull in his hand, until he had
atooned for his terrible deed by bathing in the holy pool in Varanasi
(Benares). Sometimes this wandering Shiva is depicted in a less terrifying way, and he is then known as **Kankala-Murti**. Shiva as a
beggar is the only god to wear footwear, viz., sandals.

As a god who has been cast out, Bhairava is revered particularly by
the outcastes, the untouchables.

There is a very old story about Shiva which relates how he married Rudra Uma, the daughter of Daksha. Daksha despised his son-in-law, who had no possessions, wandered around cemeteries as a naked madman, and did not show any respect for his father-in-law. Therefore he did not invite Shiva to a big sacrificial feast. Uma was filled with sorrow about this. Shiva was unable to console her by saying that, as the greatest god, he did not need any more sacrifices. Uma was unable to bear the family shame, and committed suicide. Mad with grief, Shiva plucked a hair from his head and changed it into a gigantic demon, **Virabhadra**. The demon chopped off Daksha's head. His inconsolable widow begged Shiva to reverse this deed, and Shiva reluctantly agreed. He brought Daksha back to life by placing the head of the sacrificial goat on his shoulders. In illustrations, Virabhadra is a terrifying figure, bedecked with skulls, armed to the teeth and even with two tusks protruding form the corners of his mouth. He is usually accompanied by Daksha, who can be identified by his goat's head.

Uma was reborn as **Parvati**, the daughter of Himavat, the personification of the Himalayas. At a very young age, she felt strongly attracted to Shiva. In order to win the heart of the ascetic who was constantly lost in deep meditation, she went into the mountains and meditated there for seven years.

Parvati is the shakti, or female manifestation of Shiva. She is almost always depicted together with him, either standing next to him, or sitting on his knee while the god embraces her tenderly (**Uma-Maheshvara-Murti**). Together they symbolise the twofold nature of the One Absolute. There are numerous illustrations of Shiva and Parvati as lovers, or as a married couple with their children **Skanda** and **Ganesha** in their dwelling place on Mount Kailash. There are also many stories about their tenderness, and a game of love which sometimes took months, to the irritation of the other gods.

Naturally formed lingam

The manifestation in which Shiva is most often worshipped is that of the **lingam**. There are many legends about the origin of this manifestation. In a number of these Shiva's sexual organ is first chopped off either by himself or by others, and then grows to immeasurable proportions as proof of his unimaginable strength. Another version relates how Vishnu and Brahma became embroiled in a dreadful argument about the question of who was the greatest god. In order to put an end to this, Shiva appeared between them as a flaming pillar of light to prove his supremacy. In a number of versions Brahma and Vishnu then went in search of the beginning and the end of this pillar, which took the form of Shiva's penis, and were unable to find it. Filled with awe about so much greatness, they kneeled down in front of Shiva and showed him the respect he deserved as the greatest god, the "god without beginning and without end".

Whichever legend explains the worship of the lingam, it is certainly one of the oldest ways in which Shiva is worshipped. Every Shiva temple has a "holy of holies", which is often accessible only to the truly devout or the priest. This is where Shiva's lingam is kept and worshipped, sometimes in the form of a simple stone pillar, sometimes actually in the form of a rounded lingam resting in a yoni, together forming the symbol of the fusion of male and female, creation and nourishment, the source of all life.

The rounded stone, at first in its natural form, and later specially carved, represented the formless nature of creation, even in the earliest times. As a symbol of male fertility, it embodies the all-pervasive creative force which can later be identified in the figure of the vehement storm god, Rudra. It was only possible to appease these natural forces with sacrifices, often blood sacrifices. Following the sacrificial practices relating to natural forces and the subsequent strict rituals carried out by brahmans for abstract gods, a need arose for personal gods who could also be worshipped without the intervention of a priest. It was at this point that Shiva appeared in human form. However, his lingam continued to be his most important symbol, and, like many other images of gods, it is still worshipped by covering it with red dye as a peaceful reminder of the sacrifices of earlier times. The indivisible two-in-oneness of male and female, the passive space and active time from which all life originates, is symbolized not only by the lingam and the yoni, by Shiva and his shakti, but also by the figure of the androgynous Shiva, **Ardhanarishvara**, who is half-man, half-woman.

We will conclude with the last of the many manifestations of this god without beginning and without end to be mentioned here.

Mahadeva, the greatest of all gods, in which the three gods of the Trimurti are all seen as aspects of Shiva. The three faces of this figure represent creation, preservation and destruction; or child, youth, old man; or past, present, future; or morning, noon, evening.

Sadashiva, the eternal Shiva, also known as Panchanana, "with the five faces", is depicted with five faces and often with ten arms. In this form he represents, amongst other things, the five cosmic acts: creation, preservation, destruction, concealment and salvation. A rare variation of this manifestation is that of **Mahakala**, infinite time, which can be identified by the lion on which the god is standing.

Nandi, the white bull, is the creature on which Shiva rides. As an independent deity, the bull was in ancient times the Lord of Joy (Nandikeshvara), and was represented as a man with a bull's head. Joy, i.e., music and dance, were seen as the fundamental forces of creation, an aspect which was later transferred to Shiva. Later it was said of Nandikeshvara that he was a rishi (wise man) who guarded Shiva's door to become divine in this way.

As the creature on which Shiva rides, Nandi embodies the permanent inner strength which can be acquired by controlling physical strength and violence (the name means: he who grants joy). Only those who have conquered desire and achieved self-knowledge can ride the white bull like Shiva himself.

Ganesha on his throne

Ganesha

Probably the most popular god in the Hindu pantheon is **Ganesha**, the god with an elephant's head, who is worshipped by Hindus, Buddhists and Jainists alike.

Although he is known as the eldest son of Shiva and Parvati, there are illustrations of an obviously sacred elephant which are just as old as the very first representations of a yogi, who is considered to be the precursor of the yoga god, Shiva. In fact, Ganesha is preferred to Shiva as the Lord of the Yoga by his fervent followers. His whole appearance, including the mouse on which he rides, are linked to yoga principles by these followers who see in them a symbolic significance. However, Ganesha is also a typical popular god, and in this capacity he is seen as the god of wisdom, the bringer of luck, and the clearer of obstacles. Before any journey, any ritual, or any major venture, Ganesha is first called upon and worshipped. He is married to Siddhi (Mystical Strength) and Buddhi (Insight). He is the protector of knowledge, books and education.

He is depicted as a god with a large belly, and at least four arms, seated on a lotus throne or on the mouse which he rides, or dancing. His most common attributes are the lasso, the elephant hook and a dish of sweetmeats. There is a snake in his belt.

His enormous belly symbolizes the universe. In this friendly, very earthly manifestation, and at the same time, his elevated yogic principles, he embodies a paradox: earthly delights do not have to be an obstacle to a profound spiritual insight.

There are several stories about Ganesha's birth as the child of Shiva and Parvati, and about the origin of his elephant's head. According to one popular story, Parvati was alone because Shiva had gone into retreat to meditate for a long time. She decided to make herself a son, and made him from the dust on her body before she had her daily bath. His task was to guard her door. When Shiva came home, Ganesha did not let him through either, and Shiva furiously ripped the head off his wife's obstinate guard, not realizing that it was his own son. Parvati was filled with sorrow, and Shiva consoled her with the promise that he would replace the head with the head of the very first living creature he encountered... This was an elephant. When he chopped this head off, one of the tusks broke, and therefore Ganesha has only one tusk.

As **Omkara-Ganapathi**, Ganesha clearly shows how his whole manifestation is derived from the holy sound AUM or OM, according to his yoga followers. Both in Sanskrit (left) and in Tamil (right), the written syllable OM has a pattern in which it is possible to distinguish the head and the curved trunk of Omakara-Ganapathi.

There are about ninety known manifestations of Ganesha or Ganapathi. Occasionally he has two arms, but usually there are four, and sometimes even ten. In most cases, there is only one head, but there are also manifestations with five heads.

The dancing Ganesha, **Nritya-Ganapathi**, is a special manifestation. To a casual observer this may seem rather ungainly, but in fact this dance has just as deep a significance as Shiva's cosmic dance. With the swinging movement from his left foot to his right foot, Ganesha makes the world appear and disappear. Shiva's dance may seem more varied, and above all more elegant, but this is merely the superficial choreography. Ganesha's dance reveals the heartbeat of the universe and the underlying rhythm which unites all the existing manifestations, no matter how crude or bizarre they may seem at first sight.

The god of war, **Skanda**, is the successor of Agni and Indra, who was given a new place in the pantheon as Shiva and Parvati's youngest son. There are several stories about the birth of this son. In a number of these stories, which all have a different beginning, Shiva's glowing sperm finally ends up in the Ganges to cool down, and a beautiful youth is cast up on the banks from the boiling waters. The six Pleiads in the form of nymphs, who were bathing in that spot, vied for the honour of raising the child. Then Skanda developed six heads, so that he could be breastfed by each of them. Skanda owes his other name, **Karttikeya**, to these Pleiads (Karttikas). He is described as a radiantly fair youth, extraordinarily strong, usually with six heads and sometimes with twelve arms. He carries a spear, and sometimes a bow and arrow, a lasso, wheel, shield, plough, sword, and conch shell. He rides a peacock. Skanda is particularly popular in Southern India.

Mahadevi

There are female gods in the Hindu pantheon who are the wives of the gods. They are described in this book together with their respective husbands.

However, female gods also play another independent role, and their origin can be traced back before the time of the male gods, before the arrival of the Aryans, to the time of the Mother Goddess.

In their role as wives, the goddesses are subordinate, and play a role which women have been assigned for centuries in society. They do not usually have a pronounced character like the male gods. They ride on their husband's beasts of burden, and are always depicted smaller in his company. In the Vedas, the first direct expressions of the male-oriented Aryan culture, the goddesses usually represent natural elements, such as the dawn and the night, or an aspect of fertility.

However, in popular belief, which is basically not Aryan, the Mother Goddess as a driving force of creation, has always had her followers. As the influences of popular belief increased in Hinduism, the place of this principle of god as a woman also increased. Thus there are a number of goddesses who are viewed as very independent forces, and who can sometimes even place the male god in a subordinate position.

In the Puranas, the female divine principle has a very special place. Later on, the **Tantras**, a series of books about religious and magical practices, attached great importance to the female side of the divine principle, as this is the active side or shakti.

Part of these Tantras (ritual rules) concern Radha, Vishnu's wife in his incarnation as Krishna. However, most of them are about the many manifestations of Devi, who is viewed as an independent god, but also, above all, as Shiva's shakti. Most of these Tantras are written in the form of a dialogue between Shiva and Devi, and are mainly

Temple wall in Khajuraho

concerned with the fusion of opposites, the male and female elements by means of ritual sexual acts and magical practices.

The female divine principle usually identified in general terms with the name **Devi** (goddess) or **Mahadevi** (great goddess), is worshipped in two aspects: the tender, amiable manifestations, and the terrifying, violent manifestations. This reflects the idea that, on the one hand, female strength is the source of all life, while on the other hand, it carries the destruction of life within it. In her benevolent manifestation, Devi is seen as a symbol of fertility, maternal abundance, marital fidelity, the protector of religion and art; in her terrifying manifestations she is the great protectress who guards and maintains the cosmic order as a fearless warrior.

Finally, a separate religious movement, aimed at the worship of goddesses or **Shakta**, developed from the traces of the ancient nature religions which still existed in rural areas, and the Tantras.

Amba, the world mother, a principle dating from pre-Vedic times

The Sapta Matrikas

These Seven Mother goddesses (sometimes eight are mentioned) are an independent group of goddesses who are identified with violence, disease, and human vice. They can be classified according to a system in which every goddess is linked to a male counterpart, has her own creature to ride, and represents a particular vice.

Brahmani represents pride, is linked to Brahma, and rides a goose (or swan). She has four hands and her attributes are the watering can and prayer beads.

Vaishnavi represents envy. She is linked to Vishnu, rides an eagle (Garuda), and has four or six hands. Her attributes are the wheel and conch shell.

Maheshvari represents greed. She is linked to Maheshvara (Shiva), and rides a bull. She has three eyes, four, six, or ten hands, and her attributes are a spear and prayer beads.

Indrani represents rage. She is linked to Indra, rides an elephant and has four hands. Her attributes are a bolt of lightning and a spear.

Varahi represents lust. She is linked to Varaha, the wild boar incarnation of Vishnu. She has the head of a boar and rides on a bull, or sometimes another boar. She has four hands, her attributes are a plough and a spear.

Kaumari represents bad temper. She is linked to Skanda and rides a peacock. She has three eyes and two, four or twelve arms. Her attributes are a spear and a cockerel.

Chamunda represents blindness. She is linked to Yama, and rides an owl or a corpse. She has four or ten hands, and her attributes include a spear, skull bowl, sword, shield and battle axe.

Durga is one of the most important goddesses. Originally she was worshipped as the embodiment of natural forces which grant life at the same time as taking it away. Later, she was assigned the role of the shakti of the Impersonal Absolute, the female counterpart of the male great deity. In this function she was finally also seen as the wife of Shiva in addition to, or as part of Parvati.

Durga is a very powerful goddess. In her friendly manifestation she feeds people and animals, but above all, she is the warlike protectress who always reveals her destructive strength when the earth is threatened by demons.

In exchange for her formidable powers, she demands complete subjugation from her followers and their willingness to make the ultimate sacrifice. In the past this actually involved human sacrifices, though later only animals were sacrificed to Durga.

Durga usually has eight arms, and sometimes three eyes. She sits on a lotus throne, or rides a lion or a tiger. Her attributes are a trident, sword, snake, bell, drum, shield, skull bowl, bow and arrow, wheel, club, water jug and conch shell.

One of the most important religious festivals in India is Durga Puja, which is held in October and lasts ten days. This festival is celebrated in different ways in various parts of India and different aspects play a role, but the main aim is always the worship of Shakti, the goddess as pure Power. Usually the festival celebrates Durga's victory over the buffalo demon, **Mahishashura**. This demon, who had the reputation of being an invincible giant, threatened to destroy the earth and the gods. None of the male gods could defeat him. According to one version of events, the gods together created Devi, a female god of breathtaking beauty and undaunted courage. After a bitter fight, she succeeded in killing the demon. As **Mahishashuramardini**, Durga is worshipped as the protectress of the law and destroyer of evil, and preserver of Dharma (the doctrine of divine law). During this festival, nine other manifestations of Durga, the **Nava Durgas** are worshipped, each on their own day.

Mahishashuramardini

The aspect of the Great Mother, Mahadevi, which grants life and feeds mankind, has its counterpart in the manifestation of **Kali** (the Black One). She is one of the ten **Mahavidyas**, tantric shaktis who are manifestations of the goddess **Mahakali**.

Kali is the force which governs and stops time (kala). Everything comes from her, and she devours everything. She is the embodiment of the force of destruction, divine wisdom which puts an end to all illusion.

Kali is depicted with a dark blue or even black colour. This is the colour of the earth, which also creates life through destruction. Plants die and become the nutrients for new plants, seeds are exhausted by the new life which is generated by them. Although there are depictions of Kali as a maternal goddess, she is usually depicted as an old woman, made emaciated and bony by the constant bearing and feeding of life. She has an insatiable hunger for life and devours everything in her way. She often has tusks or puts out her tongue, which is dripping with the blood of her victims. She is adorned with skulls. Sometimes she has ten heads. As Shiva's wife, she subjugates him completely, and popular representations show her dancing on his body.

In the Shakta cult, **Mahalakshmi** is the supreme goddess, the holy mother herself. She is viewed as the embodiment of the three qualities which are a precondition of the creation of life: Sattvika (purity), Tamasa (that which is hidden in the dark), and Rajasa (spiritual activity).

When the ocean of milk was churned, Mahalakshmi is said to have appeared from the foam of the seething waters, like Aphrodite. She represents Abundance, and is seen as the original mother of all life. Her followers recognize her in every goddess, and a representation of any goddess can also be a representation of Mahalakshmi. In this case she can be identified by a number of special signs. A goddess who wears a miniature lingam on her head, with three eyes and four arms, and the attributes of a coconut, vase, dish, shield and/or club in addition to the attributes of her husband, must be interpreted as a manifestation of Mahalakshmi.

Appendix

Holy places

In India a number of rivers, mountains and cities are of particular importance. A devout Hindu must visit a holy place (yatra) at least once in his life on his path to salvation from the cycle of rebirth. Below we mention a number of places, special mountains and rivers. (Also see the map on the following page.)

Rivers

Ganges	– bathing in the waters of this river absolves all sins
Jamuna	– for profound worship
Sindhu	– the river we know as the Indus

Mountains

Meru	– Brahma's heaven is on top of this mountain
Himavan	– the father of Ganga and Parvati
Mandara	– was used as the dasher to churn the ocean of milk. Durga's dwelling place.
Kailash	– Shiva's dwelling place, comparable to the Greek Mount Olympus

Cities

Benares	– the holiest of all holy places, the city of Shiva. Other names: Varanasi and Kashi.
Mathura	– Krishna's birthplace.
Dwaraka	– the capital of Krishna's realm.
Puri	– there is a statue in the temple of Jaganath which is said to be Krishna himself. Pilgrims visit this temple from all over the country, particularly during the annual Jaganathan festival.
Gaya	– a ritual for the dead which is held here grants salvation for the dead person's soul.
Ujjain	– the "navel of the earth", where there is a famous temple to Ganesha.
Haridwar	– Many places on the Ganges are sacred. Haridwar is particularly important, because this is where the Ganges flows onto the plain from the mountains. It is known as "The Gate of the Ganges".

A number of holy places and rivers in India

Marks denoting sects

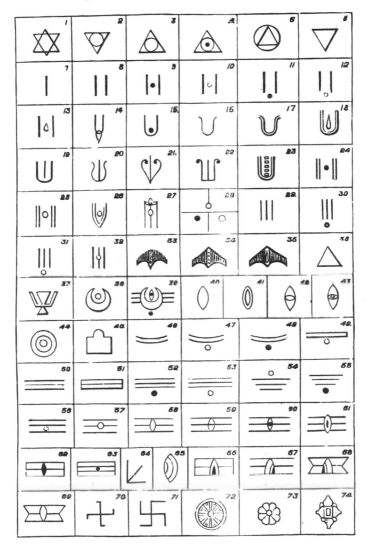

Followers of a particular sect can be identified by the mark on their forehead, arms and chest. A circle or dot is the mark of the Highest One.

Followers of Brahma and the Trimurti: numbers 1-5.

Vaishnavas, followers of Vishnu: numbers 6-35.

Saivas, followers of Shiva: numbers 36-69.

Shakti followers: number 70.

Buddhists and followers of Jainism: numbers 71-74.

Index

A

B

Bibliography

**Vier Upanishaden, Wijsheid uit het hindoeïstische Indië
– dr.Ali Beth**
Meulenhoff Amsterdam 1977

Mahabarata – Krishna Dvaipayana Vyasa
Mirananda Den Haag 1991

**De Bhagavad-Gita, zoals ze is
– A.C.Bhaktivedanta Swami Prabhupada**
The Bhaktivedanta Book Trust Amsterdam 1981

Hindoeïsme, De oudste godsdienst ter wereld – K.M.Sen
Ankh-Hermes bv Deventer 1987

India, Goden als mensen – Winand Callewaert
Davidsfonds Leuven 1991

**Die indische Götterwelt, Gestalt, Ausdruck und Sinnbild
Ein Handbuch der hinduistischen Ikonographie
– Eckard Schleberger**
Eugen Diederichs Verlag Köln 1986

The Hindu Pantheon – Edward Moor
Londen 1810 – Asian Educational Services New Delhin 1981

Hinduism, An introduction – Dharam Vir Singh
Travel Wheels Jaipur 1991

Hinduism, An Introduction – Shakunthala Jagannathan
Vakils, Feffer and Simons Ltd. Bombay 1984

Hinduism, a cultural perspective – David R. Kinsley
Prentice-Hall Inc. Englewood Cliffs, N.J. 1982

Hindu Gods and Goddesses – A.G. Mitchell
Her Majesty's Stationery Office Londen 1982

A Classical Dictionary of Hindu Mythology and Religion, Geography, History and Literature – John Dowson M.R.A.S.
Heritage Publishers New Delhi 1992

A Dictionary of Hindu Names
– Ramesh C. Dogra, Urmila Dogra
Aditya Prakashan New Delhi 1992

Hindu Mythology, Vedic & Puranic – W.J.Wilkins
Heritage Publishers New Delhi 1991

Hindu Customs and Beliefs – Shakun Narain
Bharatitya Vidya Bhavan Bombay 1987

The Industrial Arts of India Vol.1 – Dr.Birdwood C.S.I.
Chapman and Hall Ltd. Londen 1880

Shiva – Paula Fouce, Denise Tomecko
The Tamarind Press Bangkok 1990

The Riddle of Ganesha – Rankorath Karunakaran
Book Quest Bombay 1992

Ganesha, The Auspicious --- The Beginning
– Shakuntala Jagannathan, Nandita Krishna
Vakils, Feffer & Simons Ltd. Bombay 1992

With special thanks to the Royal Tropical Institute and mr. Meulenbeld, Amsterdam, and drs. Bhagwan Dutt Sukhai.

Also published in this series

Eva Rudy Jansen: The Book of Buddhas
Ritual Symbolism used on Buddhist Statuary and Ritual Objects

A brief introduction to Buddhism is followed by a lengthy survey in words and images of the most common figures, positions and symbols in Mahayana and Tantrayana Buddhism. Each individual item is clearly illustrated and accompanied by a short description of its significance. Though it does not pretend to be complete, this book is nevertheless a valuable work of reference, providing anyone who is interested with an overall iconography of a world religion and its accompanying imagery, of which the philosophy and artistry have gradually penetrated the west as well.

ISBN 978 90 74597 02 9

Ab Williams: The Complete Book of Chinese Health Balls
Practical Exercises

This book deals with an ancient Chinese fitness technique that has been in use since the Ming Dynasty (1368-1644). Two, usually metal, balls are to be moved around in the palm of the hand, thus stimulating the nervous system. These health balls are believed to improve memory, stimulate circulation, relax the muscles and tune the chi (life energy). In this book you will learn about chi and the nervous system and you will find a wide range of practical exercises that will enable you to optimise your energy. The author discusses the historical backgrounds, gives a survey of the different types of balls and their characteristics and takes you step-by-step through the basic exercises, walking and meditation exercises, and teaches you how to use the balls for massage and for strengthening the yin/yang energy in your body.

ISBN 978 90 74597 28 9

Dirk Schellberg: Didgeridoo
Ritual Origins and Playing Techniques

The didgeridoo plays an important role in the creation myths of the Australian Aborigines. The deep sound of this wind instrument helped create the world. This book describes the origins of the didgeridoo, the stories about the instrument and the players. It not only deals with Australian musicians and bands, but also discusses how Western therapists have discovered new applications for this ancient sound and shows how to build an instrument, or what to look for in purchasing one.

ISBN 978 90 74597 13 5

Eva Rudy Jansen: Singing Bowls
A Practical Handbook of Instruction and Use

The Himalayan singing bowls, also known as Tibetan or Nepalese singing bowls, are a phenomenon which is fascinating more and more westerners. By going to concerts, by undergoing so-called 'sound massages' and by experimenting themselves, people discover all sorts of possibilities and aspects of these special sounds. This book explores these possibilities and aspects, tells something about the backgrounds, and provides practical information about the way in which the bowls can be played, and how to choose a bowl for oneself. It also contains an extra chapter describing three other ritual objects: tingshaws (small cymbals), dorje (thunderbolt) and bell.

ISBN 978 90 74597 01 2